FOR RICH£R FOR P○RER

AN OXFAM REPORT ON WESTERN CONNECTIONS WITH WORLD HUNGER

BY JOHN CLARK

First published 1986
© Oxfam 1986

ISBN 0 85598 077 X

Typeset by Typo Graphics, Oxford
Printed by Belmont Press, Northampton

Published by Oxfam
274 Banbury Road, Oxford OX2 7DZ, United Kingdom.

Acknowledgements

I would like to thank the many people who helped in the preparation of this book, without whom it would never have seen the light of day.

Particular thanks go to my colleagues in Oxfam, both overseas and in the UK, who provided valuable information, suggestions and comment. Within the Campaigns Unit, special thanks go to Rob — who helped piece the initial jumble of facts, theories and ideas into a coherent shape, and to Beverley, Zita and Anne who translated the jumble into legible typescripts.

I am also very grateful to those in development institutes who provided information and guidance, in particular to Susanna Davies, Reg Green, Stephanie Griffiths-Jones, Michael Lipton, Robin Luckham, Simon Maxwell, Walter Newlyn, Andrew Nickson and Chris Smith, and to staff at the ODA, the World Bank European office, OECD and Unicef, who gave their assistance. My thanks go also to Christopher Huhne who helped me understand some of the complex issues relating to debt.

Finally, special thanks go to Sue who gave me support and encouragement when I most needed it.

John Clark,
October, 1986.

Contents

Foreword

In the winter of 1975/76 I stayed in a small village called Guriawan in the Gaya district of Bihar State, India. This is a very poor, famine prone area inhabited mostly by *harijans* or 'untouchables'. On the whole, these people are landless and are often contracted — virtually as bonded slaves — to work for the few wealthy landowners.

In general the land in this area allows two crops a year — a wheat crop from the short rains, and the main rice crop from the long monsoon rains. Over the winter, before the wheat seeds are sown, a crop of potatoes can be grown on the best land. Potatoes fill an important gap for the poor. They are cheap and readily available in the village markets during the months when rice and wheat are scarce and expensive.

The year I was there saw good harvests and there was no talk of food shortages. But by January a strange phenomenon had developed. Merchants came in droves from the town of Gaya and set up makeshift wooden shacks along the roads in the area. They were buying up potatoes. And they paid two or three times the normal price. The landlords were only too pleased to sell and for a while the main work available to the *harijans* was acting as beasts of burden, carting the potatoes to the buying points.

On 23 February 1976 I walked along with a group of them — men and women. Each had an 80lb sack perched on their head. I tried to carry one for a while but could not last more than a few hundred yards. Our journey was six miles.

When we arrived at the selling point we joined the queue. At the front was a tall, elderly man who was gaunt and thin — clearly malnourished. He scooped up the coins that the merchant slapped down on the counter and wrapped them, without checking, in his *lunghi*. He turned, and walked slowly away — slightly hunched, apparently in pain. He moved round to the side of the hut, squatting down for a rest.

Our turn in the queue came. We handed over the sacks and collected the money to take back to the landlords. As we started to walk away, the old man was struggling to his feet. We had carried on a few yards when there was a commotion behind us. Turning round, we saw people running to where the man lay, sprawled on the ground. He had simply collapsed and died. The strain of heaving that heavy sack had proved too much for him.

Tragedies like this must occur many times a day throughout India. Statistically speaking he had probably reached his full life expectancy. But here was not a statistic. Here was a real man. He had a name — Vishnath. He had a family and friends, a home, and once had a childhood. But he had no future. He died in the effort to get a bag of potatoes from point A to point B, in order to earn a few pence.

4

I felt sad, of course, but I also felt angry. Angry, because I knew that the whole sorry episode was tied up — strange as it may seem — with the potato shortage back home in Britain that year. The cause of the shortages I cannot remember, but the effect was to send the price soaring. The British, being creatures of habit, insist on potatoes with their meals, and must have chips with their fish.

The demand in Britain was met by importing from far afield; from the Canary Islands, from Egypt and now from India. The merchants were quick to seize the opportunity and that is why Vishnath carried his sack from point A to point B.

Since the export price was so good, few potatoes got to the local markets. Although the harvest had been good there was hardly a scrap of food that the landless poor could afford to buy. For the previous 5 or 6 weeks, Vishnath and his family would have lived by eating edible roots and leaves in the forest, eating an occasional rice meal on the days when there was work to be had. I know, because that was how the *harijans* of Guriawan were surviving. In this year of plenty, a massive food shortage had evolved. Vishnath was an early victim of the hunger.

Initially, it seemed wrong to me that India should be exporting food at all, especially to Britain. But that was too simplistic. India has traditionally exported tea, pulses, spices, nuts and a wealth of other foods, in exchange for the imported goods it needs from countries such as Britain. Fair exchange is no robbery. India cannot afford to be isolated within the world.

Time and time again an aid worker or a journalist will describe the irony of food exported from a region in which people go hungry. The famous Bengal famine of 1943 occurred in a year of peak food production. But food was being exported to the British troops in Burma and Singapore. During Africa's famine in 1984 journalists protested when they heard of a ship in London unloading its cargo of Ethiopian melons.

It is right to point out these ironies. They signal a real wrong. But the wrong is not the trade in Third World crops itself, but the terms of trade between the First World and the Third World, and the cruel gap in the world between rich and poor which means that the vast proportion of the benefits of trade go to the wealthy and precious little is left over for the poor.

It may make perfect sense for Kenya to switch land from growing maize for local food consumption to growing tea for export. There is an abundance of cheap maize in the world whereas tea prices, though falling, are holding up better than cereals.

But the problem is who benefits? The proceeds from selling the tea are more likely to be used on importing cars and videos, on paying interest charges on Kenya's debts rather than on importing maize for people to eat. And the price of basic food will start to rise as less is produced. This has happened in Brazil where soya, sugar, and other export crops have taken over from black beans — a staple food of the poor. The relative price of beans has shot up.

The problem is easier to define than the solution. The solution lies in attacking poverty and the forces that fuel it. Forty-four years of overseas experience has taught Oxfam that hunger rarely stems from a shortage of food, but usually from the inability of the poor to buy that food. And whether or not the food is exported, or sold in the cities, or simply stored makes little difference to the hungry.

It is not food then, that is in short supply, but justice. And to understand this lack of justice it is necessary to understand the international forces that cause hunger.

This leads into the world of macro-economics, of international trading regimes and of government policies in aid, agriculture and finance. These are complex subjects, and difficult to understand. But no-one can hide the truth. No matter how successful are the projects supported by organisations such as Oxfam, the overall war against poverty is being lost. The poor are winning some important battles, with or without outside help. But there are more hungry people in the world today than there were a decade ago.

Poverty will not be defeated just by tackling it at the micro-level, important as this work is. To stem the mounting tide necessitates attacking the root causes of poverty at the macro-level.

This book seeks to explain some of those international root causes, and to suggest how they could be tackled. It addresses the role of Western governments — the British government in particular — in contributing to this endeavour.

Clearly the causes of poverty are by no means the monopoly of Western governments. There are many contributory factors. Governments, landowners and business elites of Third World countries themselves have the ultimate power to decide how wealth is shared amongst their people. All too often they annex benefits of economic growth for themselves and show scant interest in the welfare of their poor. While some governments are progressive and caring, others rarely seem to act in the interests of their people. Transnational corporations in their turn wield enormous power over farming systems, employment and trade in developing countries and so control the destiny of millions of people. And the Soviet bloc has immense influence in many developing countries.

Each of these issues could be the subject of a further book, so the focus of this book is deliberately restricted to the role of the British and other Western governments. Although only part of the picture, it is a part where we can at least exercise some influence.

Vishnath's death is over ten years ago now. I still remember it clearly, but sometimes it seems rather removed from the complex world of politics and international trade. The two are connected, I know. His fate lay in the fact that he was an unequal partner in international trade. It seems to me that, for Vishnath, the problem lay in a sudden shift to export food that had previously been a staple of the poor.

This book seeks to show how our daily lives in Britain are intertwined with millions of people like Vishnath. We may not see them, but they are our neighbours as surely as if they lived in the next street: how we lead our lives affects the way they are able to lead theirs. That is why we must look carefully at British policies that affect the Vishnaths of this world, and see what can be done to improve the supply of justice.

INTRODUCTION
Setting the Scene

No-one needs reminding of the famine in Africa. In 1986 several million African people are still severely threatened by it. They have become regular visitors to our homes through TV documentaries. Theirs is the "loud emergency", but famine is just the tip of the iceberg. Below the surface are more than 700 million people living in a state of malnutrition. One in six of the human race. Fifteen million children die as a result of poverty every year.[1]

Every other second another child quietly dies. Theirs is the "silent emergency".

The number of malnourished people in Africa has risen from 80 to 100 million since 1980.[2] South of the Sahara more than a quarter of all children under five are malnourished. There is record suffering in a world which has the resources, the knowledge and the technical ability to eradicate hunger for ever. But this capacity is not being used. Instead the wealthier countries are pursuing economic policies which deepen the crisis of hunger and poverty. World economic policies, led by the major industrialized countries, have conspired to squeeze dry the economies of most developing countries.

Western aid for famine relief is well publicised, and deservedly so. **Through public goodwill and government action some three and a half billion dollars was provided for the African relief effort in 1985. But virtually unreported was the fact that in the same year the 29 poorest countries in Africa paid back to the industrialised countries TWICE this amount in payments on their debts (see Appendix I).**

In 1984 Oxfam launched a new movement *"Hungry for Change"*. This is a movement of British people who find the current levels of world hunger and poverty intolerable and who believe that the action taken by governments such as our own is woefully inadequate in the face of such suffering. Moreover the movement seeks to understand, publicise and find alternatives to the way in which current economic and trade policies pursued by the wealthier countries actually DEEPEN this crisis.

Through these policies Western governments are exporting our problems of recession. As a recent UNICEF survey of a wide range of countries has shown, the impact of world recession is being passed on from industrialised to developing countries, then from the wealthier to the poorer people in those countries.[3] At each step the effects are multiplied rather than diminished.

An Oxfam survey in Ceara, N. E. Brazil, in 1983 showed that child malnutrition stood at a staggering 40% as a result of the dual crisis of debt and drought.[4]

Celebrity launch of Oxfam's Hungry for Change Campaign in October, 1984.

'Debt and Poverty in Jamaica' a 1985 Oxfam report describes how 40% of all export earnings of that country were consumed by its debt service bill and how this, coupled with the falling world price of bauxite, led to a rise in food prices, a drop in wages and a sharp increase in malnutrition, with 28% of children under four malnourished.[5] Similarly, Oxfam's report on Sudan lists debt as an underlying cause of famine in that country.[6]

Oxfam staff in many countries have linked a rapid escalation of poverty to international economic policies. But not only Oxfam makes the link. UNICEF, for example, paint this gloomy picture of Ghana:

"The percentage of malnourished children in Ghana has risen sharply in the 1980s, now standing at a staggering 53%. In 1984, 56% of Ghana's foreign exchange was spent on debt service, and this necessitated massive cuts in essential imports, hitting health (especially imported drugs and medical equipment), education (teaching materials) and water supplies (40% of the country's water supply systems, especially in the rural areas, have broken down for lack of fuel and essential equipment). The infant mortality rate in Ghana, which had been declining over 15 years, has risen from 100 per thousand in 1980 to between 120 and 130 in 1985. There can be no doubt that this is a cruel consequence of the debt crisis".[7] Oxfam's West Africa office echoes this and says that the economic problems have contributed to a serious brain drain in Ghana. While there were 1,655 doctors practising there in 1981, by 1985 this number had fallen to 817.[8]

International economic forces have, in addition, contributed to the following catalogue of human tragedies, by weakening and distorting national economies, reducing foreign exchange needed for imports and forcing cuts in social services spending.

8

- **Brazil** — an increase in low birthweight babies and an increasing proportion of infant deaths resulting from malnutrition.
- **Sri Lanka** — a marked increase in wasting amongst children since the mid 1970s.
- **Costa Rica** — a doubling of the number of children treated for severe malnourishment over the last three years.
- **Zambia and Chile** — a 30–40% drop in household incomes since 1980.
- **Mozambique** — no foreign exchange for importing essential drugs.
- **Zimbabwe** — a 20% cut in social services spending.

The problem is not a shortage of food, but an inability of the poor to buy or grow enough food for a healthy life. It is a problem of food security — a problem which cannot be solved merely by technological advances which improve farm yields. Poor people need access to land and inputs for food-growing. They must have surpluses to store from harvest time until the lean season; employment so they can earn enough to buy sufficient food; welfare schemes as a 'safety net'. In short, the solution to hunger is not so much technological as political.

This has been recognised by a recent report from the World Bank — an organisation usually more concerned with world economic growth than hunger and poverty. *"The world has ample food"* says the report, *"we now need to realise that, in the global sense, and often in individual countries, an adequate food supply is no longer the source of the problem . . . from among the many forces that conspire to leave almost one person in five in today's world underfed, one stands out about all others: poverty".*[9]

The report goes on to describe new principles which the World Bank and other agencies should pursue if the food security of the poor is to be improved. These principles might mean, *"shifting resources from large farms to small farms, from export crops to food crops, from industry to agriculture and from capital intensive to labour intensive activities".*

None of this is particularly new. Oxfam and other development agencies have been saying much the same thing for years and the World Bank itself advocated an 'aid for the poorest' strategy in the early 1970s. But now at least some in this powerful organisation are once again calling for the eradication of poverty and hunger as a World Bank priority.

The immediate human crisis is one of hunger and poverty. But the seeds of tomorrow's crisis — perhaps a far worse one — are already sown. The rapid destruction of the environment could have a cataclysmic effect on generations to come. A population concerned about daily survival, which has to spend several hours per family in search of fuel-wood, is not one which nurtures and cares for its forests. Governments plagued with crippling interest bills are not careful stewards of their natural resources. The concentration on export crop farming and on timber used to offset oil imports is costing the environment dearly. Each year some 40,000 square miles of forest land is lost — equivalent to the land area of Scotland and Wales.[10] At this rate one fifth of the world's remaining tropical forests will be gone by the end of the century. Africa has already lost half of its forests during this century.

Moreover over-working of already eroded land has a heavy cost. The poor

Each year some 40,000 square miles of forest land are lost.

cannot afford to leave land fallow. They cannot afford fertilisers, and they do not have the animals to manure the land. The soil is not allowed to regenerate and the protective top cover is not restored. Water and wind erosion gradually thin the topsoil and every year, world-wide, 80,000 square miles of once fertile land declines to a point where it will no longer yield anything. The pressure to survive today is creating the deserts of tomorrow.

It is the list of silent emergencies which makes it so important to look closely at the policies pursued by Western governments. It is vital to examine the impact of these policies on the poor of the world and to change them when they contribute to world hunger.

The *'Hungry for Change'* campaign identifies five main policy areas which need addressing: government aid policies, international trade, Western agricultural policies, the handling of the debt crisis and finally the arms trade with the Third World. Each is the subject of one of the following chapters.

AID

Getting it Right

One of Oxfam's most experienced partners in Africa, Sithembiso Nyoni of Zimbabwe, addressed Oxfam's national conference in 1985. She reminded her audience that, *"Britain didn't overcome its Dickensian poverty of the 19th century by a multitude of development projects"*. European poverty, she pointed out, was controlled by social and economic reform, not by aid.

The industrial revolution and rapid economic growth had provided a good foundation of national wealth in Britain and Europe in the nineteenth century, but it was a long series of political disputes, the work of social reformers and the organisation of Trade Unions that enabled the poor to get a larger share of this national wealth. Overseas aid didn't enter the picture.

In the 20th century, however, aid has played a part in overcoming poverty. Aid from the USA — the Marshall plan — was the key in helping war-torn Europe back onto its feet. But even now aid is a small part of the world's economy, and it cannot solve the problems of poverty. It can help — particularly with specific problems. But poverty will continue to haunt the world until the underlying causes are dealt with. This calls for reforms in the developing countries — for a narrowing of the gap between rich and poor, between the powerful and the powerless and between men and women. And it also calls for international reforms, especially in trade and finance.

Because aid necessarily has a limited role, it is particularly important to target it carefully at the needs of the very poor.

On the whole aid through the voluntary agencies is more successful at achieving this than *official aid* — the aid given by the richer governments. Official aid, however, is about seven times the volume of voluntary aid, so it's important to get it right.

Official aid and development

The wealthier countries of both East and West and most OPEC countries have a government aid budget. These funds are given (or occasionally lent at subsidised interest rates — increasingly uncommon for British aid) to governments of poorer countries. The aid may be given directly (bilateral) or via an international or 'multilateral' agency such as the World Bank, the UN agencies and the EEC. A small proportion of it may be channelled through voluntary agencies such as Oxfam or through international research institutes,

...t the rest goes to overseas governments for agreed 'development' schemes.

The word 'development' covers a multitude of ideas — not just the relief of poverty. Recent British government aid grants demonstrate this variety.[1]

■ £190 million went for emergency relief in Africa from 1984–6.

■ £65 million provided Westland helicopters for India.

■ £2.2 million helped extend the primary health care service to poor people in the remoter parts of Orissa State, India.

■ £7 million built a new hospital in the Falkland Islands.

■ £18 million paid for a new repair yard to replace the naval dockyard in Gibraltar.

'Development' — in official aid language — is more about economics than people. Helping people break out of poverty is 'development', but so too are schemes, such as airports, that help the Third World elite. These schemes contribute to economic growth and so, the theory goes, the country as a whole benefits — not just the elite. It is Oxfam's experience, however, that the benefits of this sort of 'development' rarely reach the poor unless the government in question is determined to make this happen, or unless the development scheme is carefully designed to reflect the needs of the poor.

Oxfam is concerned with people, not economic indicators such as per capital Gross National Product (GNP). Life expectancy and nutrition standards are much more important than balance of trade statistics. History shows that it is difficult to achieve better living standards for the poor without the foundation of a reasonably healthy national economy. But national prosperity by no means automatically leads to individual survival. Desperate levels of poverty co-exist with opulence in some of the world's wealthier countries, such as South Africa. The poor need justice as much as they need economic growth.

The key problem is that official aid to a very poor country may help the elite without touching the poor. It may even leave the poor worse off, for instance when farm mechanisation puts labourers out of work. In the same way aid can widen the gaps within the family. Aid projects based on the assumption that the benefits will automatically flow equally to men and women almost inevitably find that the men annex most of the gain.

'Getting it right' involves learning from past experiences of aid successes and failures. But above all it involves deciding that the purpose of aid is to help the poorest — men *and* women. And that is a political choice.

British aid

Britain's aid is handled by the **Overseas Development Administration** (ODA) under the Minister for Overseas Development.

Bilateral aid accounts for about 60% of the budget, and multilateral aid about 40%. The use of bilateral aid is mutually agreed between the two governments

Desperate poverty co-exists with opulence — a shanty area on the fringes of Recife, Brazil.

— donor and recipient. Aid is a shared responsibility, but the donor — holding the purse strings — inevitably wields a lot of power.

Most bilateral aid is **'tied'** — that is, given in the form of British goods or services (such as a contract to a British construction company to build a road). A serious criticism of tied aid is that not only does it encourage concentration on large projects and inappropriate aid, but it can also help bolster up inefficient British companies. It is estimated that the tying of aid reduces its value by 20–40%.[5] The remainder of bilateral aid is **'untied'** — in cash. Most of this would be spent within the developing country as **'local costs'**, such as paying for an agricultural training scheme.

Quantity of aid

While hunger persists, can aid ever be enough? It is impossible to walk through an emergency feeding centre in Ethiopia and believe that governments of the

Case Study — Sudan

Sudan is one of the poorest nations on Earth, and faces a chronic problem of hunger. Any aid — particularly supporting agriculture — would appear to make sense.

However, a 1986 Oxfam report, 'Sudan: the Roots of Famine', describes how Sudan is a very divided society where certain help to agriculture can hurt the poor.[2]

Sudan has been the scene of many aid funded large irrigation schemes, notably the Gezira project, and more recently the Kenana sugar complex. These schemes open up tracts of land, once used for grazing cattle, to modern farming. The original settlers are cleared off the land and often the traditional routes followed by nomads are blocked off. The farming methods are highly mechanised, and very few of the displaced people are able to earn wages from the scheme. One tractor, probably paid for by aid, takes the jobs of several people.

Instead, the elite benefit. A small band of wealthy farmers — usually retired soldiers, businessmen and merchants — are able to make a fortune, often with the help of foreign aid. The environment is degraded, as trees are hacked down to give way to more fields, and most of the crops grown are sold in the cities (sorghum) or exported (cotton and groundnuts). Poor people — who get no employment from these schemes — simply cannot afford the high prices fixed by the powerful cartel of grain merchants.

The monopoly of these merchants has been strengthened by the recent famine. In 1986 the EEC decided to buy famine relief food in the food surplus areas of Sudan rather than supply European food aid, as had been world are doing 'enough'. But aid is just one of the many claims on a government's limited power to spend. So perhaps the question should be, *"what priority does our government give to aid, and how does this compare with other governments?"*.

The usual measurement for comparing the size of governments' aid programmes is the percentage of the country's Gross National Product (GNP) given as aid. There is a recognised target set by the United Nations of 0.7% GNP, yet reached by very few countries.

The British government maintains that its official aid programme (accounting for 0.34% of GNP) compares favourably with that of other Western governments in the OECD (which totalled 0.35% in 1985). This comparison is defective on two counts.

Firstly, it ignores the fact that British aid levels since 1960 have been way *ahead* of world aid levels and that since 1979 they have fallen steeply as world levels have been maintained or even increased. Chart A illustrates the rise and fall of UK aid.

---

done the previous year. This was a move welcomed by Oxfam. But Oxfam's representative in Sudan quickly saw that the commercial elite of Kassala Province and elsewhere were making a fortune selling grain to the EEC at inflated prices.[3] This strengthens the hold of the elite, and yet their farming methods are very inefficient. Large surpluses were produced only because of the vast areas farmed. Again, aid has helped a farming system which excludes the poor.

The British government has started funding the Equatoria Regional Agricultural Programme designed to help smallholders, but it accounts for a minute proportion of the Sudan aid programme (£5 million in 1984). From 1980—84 UK aid to Sudan totalled £154 million, of which nearly half (£74 million) was spent on building a power station for the capital city, Khartoum.[4]

John Selwyn Gummer — then Conservative Party Chairman — admitted in a TV interview that *"we don't like such schemes"*, but argued that it is for such projects that Third World governments seek funding.

Since the debt crisis began to bite in the early 1980s and the International Monetary Fund (IMF) imposed austerity measures on countries which could not keep up with their debt repayments, the poor have become poorer. Subsidies on food or fuel were cut and government spending on social services pared back.

Against this background existing official aid practice appears inadequate. The main emphases are irrigation schemes, mechanised farming, dams, roads and urban electricity supplies which have no direct relevance to the people living in famine prone areas.

% GNP allocated as aid (net disbursements) 1960–1985

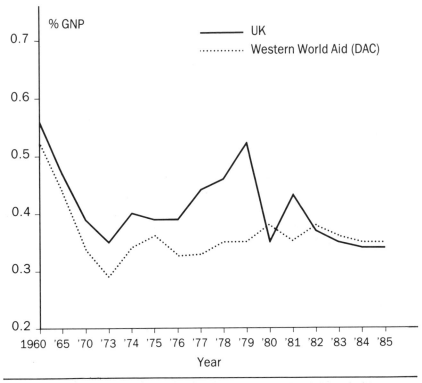

The 'Western World Aid' is the average of the member states of the Development Assistance Committee (DAC) of the Organisation for Economic Co-operation and Development (OECD).

But even this picture is deceptive, because the Western World figures give undue prominence to one country. The USA is such a huge economy that a decline in its aid programme — as we've seen in recent years — gives the false impression that the whole Western world is turning against aid. Chart B shows how British aid compares with the aid level for the Western world *less* the USA (0.45% GNP in 1985). It shows how other Western nations have steadily increased their aid levels since the early 1970s and how British aid was ahead of the field from 1976–79, but has fallen dramatically behind since then. Superimposed on the same chart is the aid level for other countries in the EEC. This comparison makes the British performance appear all the more disappointing. While our closest political and economic allies have seen fit to forge further ahead of the rest of the world in terms of aid performance, British aid has taken a nosedive.

Chart B

% GNP allocated as aid (net disbursements) 1960–1985

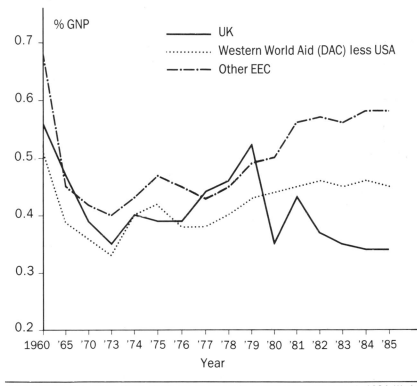

Source: OECD data; 1960–1983, OECD *Development Co-operation* (various issues); 1984, World Bank *World Development Report 1985;* 1985, ODA, 1985 Annual Report.

Britain would have to increase its aid programme by 70% in order to come back in line with the EEC (0.58% GNP in 1985). Furthermore, our Commonwealth allies (Canada, Australia and New Zealand) are also beating Britain, giving in total 0.48% GNP as aid in 1985.

Britain's aid has been cut dramatically in comparison with other Western countries. In money terms the aid programme sounds large. In the financial year 1986/7 the net budget is £1,187 million. But this is less than 1% of the government's overall budget and is a level which has fallen in real terms by about a fifth over the past seven years.

As Third World poverty has deepened, British aid has been cut back significantly, although after a record breaking mass lobby of Parliament in October 1985 the aid budget was revised upwards by £17 million. This was a welcome shift, but nowhere near enough to make up for seven years of cuts.

Campaigning for increased British overseas aid — a record-breaking lobby of Parliament in 1985.

Ironically the famine in Africa — which did so much to increase the awareness of the general public — served to reduce the budget for long-term development. Thousands of people wrote asking the government to give more famine relief and there were several parliamentary debates. The Aid Minister responded to this pressure with a series of emergency grants. But this was not, on the whole, new money. It came out of existing aid funds intended for *development* elsewhere rather than emergency relief. The all-party Foreign Affairs Committee of the House of Commons criticised the government on this point, arguing that central government contingency reserves should be used to help tackle such major disasters.[6] One result of the shift in aid to African famine relief has been the sharp decline in UK aid to other regions. In particular, aid to the Indian sub-continent fell from £237 million in 1984 to £193 million in 1985.

Quality

The quality of aid is even more important than the quantity. The crucial question is, how effectively does aid improve the living standards of the very poor? In Britain its effectiveness is reduced by a conflict between the ideals of relieving poverty and British self-interest. In particular:

— political concerns influence how much aid goes to which countries;

— commercial interests determine the form of aid given and the nature of projects supported;

— embarrassing agricultural surpluses determine how EEC food aid is given.

Political interests

All governments use political criteria in allocating aid. In the case of Britain this 'politicisation' is exaggerated by its colonial connections and overseas dependencies. Hence in 1985, in spite of massive public and media concern about famine in Africa, Gibraltar, with a population of about 27,000 received almost as much UK aid as Ethiopia, with 40 million people, mostly extremely poor. In 1985 the Falkland Islands received the equivalent of £5,500 per person of UK aid, while India received 15p per person. While it may be the case that these British Dependencies need the facilities provided, the costs should not be charged to the overseas aid budget.

For political and commercial reasons, more British aid has gone to wealthier countries such as Turkey, Mexico and the Philippines during the 1980s than to a number of more obviously needy countries.

Political criteria can be seen most clearly in the case of Central America. A decade ago Britain gave considerable aid to the Somoza dictatorship in Nicaragua. Now, since the change in regime, that aid has been all but cut off. Costa Rica and Honduras received respectively 40 times and 87 times as much UK aid per person as did Nicaragua in 1983, and the disparity was even greater in 1984.[9]

The ODA has stated a policy of, *"a greater focus of aid . . . where local policies seemed likely to be supportive of aid efforts"*[10] and has recognised that Nicaragua has *"a good record of spending development aid"*.[11] Oxfam has considerable experience of the effectiveness of humanitarian assistance in Nicaragua, but in spite of this the country is effectively denied British aid.

It is true that Nicaragua is not one of the poorest countries in the world, and it could be argued that other countries are more in need of aid, but there are many countries wealthier than Nicaragua which do get substantial British aid. Moreover, the destabilisation and destruction caused by the continuing guerilla war has meant that many communities in Nicaragua face immense hardship. Despite political difficulties, there is plenty of scope for humanitarian assistance, and in Oxfam's experience, the Nicaraguan government is doing more to help its people than many other governments to whom Britain is more generous.

Similarly, the British government is unwilling to give aid to Kampuchea. Again, there are difficult political obstacles. The United Nations continues to recognise a government in exile, formerly led by Pol Pot, as the legitimate leaders and sees the ruling government of Heng Samrin as a Vietnamese puppet. But despite the obstacles, the urgent needs of the Kampuchean people should dictate a generous humanitarian response.

In Ethiopia the British government abandoned development aid in the late 1970s because it was perceived as ineffective and simply supporting a Soviet style government. However, even in such circumstances it is possible to use development aid in ways that benefit the poor, and do not 'prop up' regimes which are not favoured by the British government. Oxfam put forward a proposal for this type of development aid to Ethiopia — a proposal welcomed by the UK ambassador in Addis Ababa.[12] Eventually the government did agree to a £3 million programme similar to that outlined by Oxfam, concentrating on rural water supplies, seeds, soil and water conservation and farm tools.

Because so much UK aid is allocated according to political criteria, there is little left over for the poorest countries which have less political or commercial clout. So UK aid to the so-called 'least developed' countries, like Bangladesh and Tanzania, fell from 0.14% of GNP in 1981 to 0.08% in 1984.[13] Total aid from all countries to sub-Saharan Africa has stagnated at $9 billion per year, while debt repayments have risen from $2.3 billion to $8 billion.[14]

Commercial interests

Three quarters of British bilateral aid is 'tied' to UK goods and services. Naturally, if an aid programme requires imported machinery, and a suitable British product is available at a competitive price, the ODA would want to supply that rather than, say, a Japanese alternative. Many tools, pumps, specialised equipment, metals, fertilisers, vehicles and spare parts need to be imported. Sometimes research workers or technical expertise need to be brought in. All of these can be provided by official aid — and they provide jobs and contracts in Britain too. But at present there is such a heavy emphasis on tied aid that the aid programme appears to be more concerned with supporting ailing sectors of British industry than the Third World poor.

Britain was criticised recently for tying more of its aid than other donors, but the knots are being tied still tighter.[15] In March 1986, for example, a £65 million aid deal was finalised with India for 21 Westland W-30 helicopters, intended for offshore oil exploration work. Each one of these helicopters costs more to the aid budget than the whole development programme for Ethiopia.

The Indian government did not want to accept this aid — but agreed reluctantly when told that they were unlikely to get the aid otherwise. It was the helicopters or nothing.

The scheme was disliked by many within the ODA. Nonetheless, it came about because the government wanted to help the ailing Westland company. £65 million (more than the annual budget of Oxfam) was spent at a stroke.

Oxfam staff in India have argued that other UK aid schemes, such as airport surveillance equipment and the provision of a new traffic light system in Calcutta, are low priority for the millions of people who are still hungry in India.

If official aid simply couldn't help the poor it wouldn't be so bad. But elsewhere in India there are innovative ODA schemes for improving health services (Orissa), for improving nutrition (Gujarat) and for increasing the yields of small farmers through improved fertiliser use (East India). Aid such as this, especially in the form of local costs, can 'reach the parts other aid doesn't'. It is this kind of aid — not helicopters — that most taxpayers want to see their money spent on. It is 'Real Aid'.

The most commercial aspect of British aid is the so-called Aid Trade Provision (ATP) — in essence a subsidy for UK exporters.

ATP was created by a Labour government in 1978, but has been greatly

Enough Said?

Frankly, there's been more than enough said about Westland over the past few months.

This ad is not about politics, it's not about recriminations, it's simply about success. What's more, success for the newly recapitalised Westland plc.

Two days ago the contract signed recently, to supply 21 Westland 30's to the Helicopter Corporation of India became effective. Three year's negotiation is over, two years of manufacture is about to begin. For an order worth over £65 million.

At the moment we've little else to say. (And anyway, if you'll excuse us, we've got work to do.)

WESTLAND
Westland plc Yeovil England

This advertisement which recently appeared in the national press totally fails to mention one fact: far from being a triumph to Westland salesmanship, this £65 million order was almost wholly paid for not by the Indians but by the British aid budget. Enough said?

Source: WDM, *Spur,* May 1986.

expanded in recent years. A company, seeking to win a lucrative contract in a developing country — say to build a steel mill — can apply to the Department of Trade and Industry (DTI) for help. The DTI may estimate that perhaps £10 million will clinch the deal against a foreign competitor. The DTI then approaches the ODA to ask for an ATP subsidy. The ODA usually has to make a snap judgement, having no time to look at the social aspects of the project.

As the former head of the ODA, Sir William Ryrie, has said of the ATP, *"the borderline between aid to developing countries and aid to British industry is sometimes hard to find".*[16]

Examples of ATP projects agreed in 1984 include £33 million for a GEC built power station in India, £5.3 million for the UK construction giant, UKAG, to build an airport in Sri Lanka, and £6.7 million for power lines in Jordan and Indonesia.

A TV documentary in 1985 described one ATP project. A Midlands company — Willowbrook — won an ATP funded contract to supply bus bodies and chassis to Zambia. This was against the advice of British High Commission staff in Zambia, who thought that the buses wouldn't stand the rough road conditions. They were right. The buses broke down very quickly, the Zambian government was furious, but the company had by this time gone into receivership.

Food aid — good and bad

In the summer of 1984 Oxfam made its largest ever grant for sending a shipload of food to Ethiopia, announcing at the time that it was taking this step to shame the British and other governments into committing relief aid to a major famine. But it was not until November of that year, when harrowing pictures of the famine made the headlines of TV news bulletins and a public clamour arose, that major international relief efforts were launched by governments. In the words of Foreign Office Minister, Tim Eggar, *"the famine had become a domestic political issue"* to which the government had to respond.

The British government took the lead in mounting a concerted EEC food aid effort in December 1984. Though dwarfed by the scale of the famine, this emergency food aid undoubtedly saved thousands of lives.

Food aid such as this is vitally needed, but in other circumstances it can be a handicap for the poor. The bulk of food aid is not used in emergencies and, as a former head of the ODA said, *"is frankly more a means of disposing of European agricultural surpluses than of helping the poor".*[17]

Food aid is the subject of lively debate. There are four principal issues:

Speed — the EEC responded only slowly to the famine in Africa. Oxfam and other organisations had warned of impending famine, sophisticated 'early warning systems', contributed to by British government funds, had been signalling a red alert for many months, but it was only when television brought the famine to everyone's homes that governments began to take serious action.

Even when it is decided to provide food aid, EEC procedures are often very slow. Oxfam staff in Mali, for instance, describe how food aid arrived up to four months late. By the time it arrived, it coincided with the best harvest for five

'Real Aid' such as support for community health programmes 'reaches the parts other aid doesn't'.

years. As there was then so much food available, market prices remained extremely low and the poor farmers were hit.[18]

A similar picture emerges from Burkina Faso, where Oxfam staff report that with food aid still on sale in the markets, producer prices have been held down and warehouses are bursting with grain.

Oxfam has recently issued a report proposing an important series of reforms to EEC food aid procedures so that there is a much swifter response to emergencies in future.[19] The former UK Aid Minister has given his personal support to the majority of these proposals.

Food aid use — the EEC's annual food aid programme is very large, but in most years only about a tenth of this goes to famine relief. The bulk is given to governments who sell it commercially or use it in state institutions such as hospitals. Little goes directly to the poor and in fact can actually harm them. In forcing local food prices down, food aid can make life difficult for small farmers, and can encourage Third World governments to place less emphasis on improving their countries' agriculture.

However, there is no clear-cut answer to these problems. Some countries, particularly in Africa, are dependent on food imports, and if they can get them free through food aid, this clearly saves precious foreign exchange. The key rests in providing food aid as part of an overall *food strategy* for the country in question, designed to help strengthen, not undermine, the local farming and marketing structures. EEC aid is now beginning to move in this direction.

Country allocation — at present the distribution of food aid bears little relation to need. In 1985 — the peak famine year — only about 20% of the EEC's food aid went on famine relief, and Egypt received more EEC food aid than Ethiopia.

Quantities and kind — the amounts of food aid given are strongly related to the EEC's problem of food mountains. Half the value of EEC food aid, therefore, is not wheat or other basic grain, but milk powder and butter oil, which generally proves to be inappropriate. In spite of all such evidence, the European Commission has recently proposed an *increased* share of dairy produce in food aid. In June 1986, however, the UK Aid Minister — citing Oxfam evidence — announced his intention to use his influence within the EEC to reform food aid and in particular to 'de-link' it from the EEC problem of agricultural surpluses.[20]

Opportunity

Official aid can help the very poor. But it can also create problems for them. Or it can exaggerate existing imbalances within their communities, notably between men and women. Given the problems, how can official aid be most effective?

Involving the poor

In Oxfam's experience the key to effective aid — and this applies equally to official and non-governmental, or voluntary, aid — is devising schemes that the poor themselves see as the answer to their problems. This means consulting poor people in the design and execution of projects, and working with local structures that genuinely represent them.

'Popular participation' is a favourite slogan of development workers today. It is easy to claim as a principle, but it is immensely difficult to achieve — even for non-governmental organisations like Oxfam. For official aid agencies it is very much more difficult, because they channel aid largely to Third World governments who, understandably, dislike strings and conditions being attached. Targeting and involving poor people may seem a reasonable condition for aid, but to governments it can often appear as unwarranted interference. For example, they might not wish to allow a donor government to send in people to discuss future projects with poor communities because it would represent an abdication of local governmental responsibility.

Official aid should form a 'partnership for development' with a Third World government. In a scheme such as providing credit to poor farmers this might mean strengthening existing structures; extending bank or co-operative services for example, or it might mean creating new structures — village based revolving loan schemes, perhaps. Either way, it would have to be a joint undertaking between the two partners. In some countries this is easier to achieve than in others. Some governments are 'pro-poor' and have a decentralised approach which favours this type of partnership. Others are completely hostile to such ideas. Most fall somewhere between, with some progressive ministries or departments which can be persuaded to employ the 'partnership' approach.

The starting point is to agree that a major proportion of official aid should be spent on projects which directly alleviate poverty. In December 1985 Britain and India reached an important agreement that at least 20% of all cash aid to India should be as local costs for this type of project.[21] However, in any such agreement, the problem remains of how best to consult and involve poor people themselves. Heeding only the advice of existing leaders may do no more than to reinforce the power of a local elite. Official aid projects which have been successful in reaching the poor have often started by creating new mechanisms for involving people, such as village meetings and women's groups, but this takes time and great care. Local voluntary organisations can usually help, but it is important not to overload these groups, distort them into bureaucracies or otherwise corrupt them.

As many official aid agencies try to do more to help the poor *directly*, popular participation will become an increasingly important area of debate and experiment. It could prove to be the meeting ground between voluntary and official agencies which both describe their work as aid, but until now have been involved in quite different processes.

Women in development

Listening to the voice of the poor by itself is not enough. Usually, that is a male voice. Development projects which improve the economy of a community may well benefit the men but leave the women and children worse off than before. A classic mistake of development is to assume that the poor live in nuclear families and that to benefit the male head of the household is to benefit all members of the family. In reality there is usually a tremendous wealth gap within the family. The men own the property and eat better. A development approach that assumes the 'household' as the unit of development also does not recognise that more than one third of all households are headed by women.

Projects which offer employment may encourage men to move from their homes, leaving the women to look after the children and household and earn their keep. Agricultural schemes may encourage production for sale rather than domestic use. In these examples, the men will receive the cash and frequently very little goes to other members of the family. An Oxfam paper on this subject describes the frequent occurrence of malnourished women and children while the men sport new clothes, bicycles and radios.[22]

Malawi is often quoted as a shining example of development. It has achieved considerable growth and economic reform. Yet only 4% of its women can read and write, and it has the fifth highest infant mortality rate in the world.

If a development project is to be relevant to women, they too must be consulted and actively involved in the project. However, social and cultural practice often makes it difficult for development workers — the majority of whom are men — to meet the women of a community. Priorities for both official and voluntary aid agencies are to appoint more women staff, to explore all avenues of consulting with poor women and to devise more projects which specifically address the needs of women. For example, in most developing countries women do the majority of the farming, yet few receive training or

If a development project is to be relevant to women, they too must be consulted.

support from existing projects. Experience shows that when women are involved, not only are the projects more successful, but the benefits go to *all* members of the family, especially the children.

In Zambia Oxfam funds agricultural training and advice centres for women because existing services effectively exclude them, although 40% of rural households are headed by women.[23]

Basic services

Basic human needs are often neglected in favour of prestige urban development schemes. This is particularly acute in Africa, according to Unicef, since the overall economic diffculties of that region have led to a serious decline in basic services such as health and education.[24] Unicef calls for a 'floor under poverty' approach so that all, however poor, have access to health care, water supplies and basic education. Simple measures exist which could have saved millions of lives; immunisation against the major killer diseases, treatment of diarrhoea with salt and sugar rehydration solutions and a small range of essential drugs. The infrastructure needed to support these measures — health and education services in even the remotest areas, for example — is, however, expensive to set up and maintain; beyond the reach of many poor countries. Much more official aid should be used to establish these vital basic services.

Agricultural development

The famine in Africa has sparked off a timely international debate about whether official aid is doing enough to prevent hunger and whether it could do more. The House of Commons Foreign Affairs Committee has called on the British government to increase this type of aid. The government agreed that it was important to respond to the 'changing needs of Africa' and the Aid Minister agreed on, *"the importance of doing all we can to help the smaller farmers in African countries and in other parts of the world who face difficulties"*. One of the main challenges for future UK aid, he said, *"is to look much more closely at what can be done to revitalise peasant agriculture"*.

This is an important policy statement. Up until 1984 the trend in British aid certainly wasn't in this direction. In 1984 only 16% of UK bilateral aid went to agriculture. The All Party Parliamentary Group on Overseas Development published a report in 1985 called 'UK Aid to African Agriculture', which showed that the real value of such aid had fallen by about one third between 1979 and 1984.[27] The report also revealed increased commercial criteria, diverting aid from direct benefits (such as crops, livestock and forestry) towards indirect, infrastructural aid, such as roadbuilding by British construction industries.

Moreover, the tendency is to focus aid on the more productive areas rather than the vulnerable regions. For example in Sudan considerable UK aid has gone to a massive irrigation scheme in Gezira, producing mainly cotton, rather than on small-scale irrigation for subsistence farming in the famine prone areas of Darfur and Kordofan. Small-scale irrigation can help increase staple food production and is of immense benefit to subsistence farmers. But official aid usually favours the jumbo schemes. So, although two thirds of all irrigated land in sub-Saharan Africa is found in Sudan, notably in Gezira, large areas of the country are gripped by famine.[28]

The All Party Group report showed that two thirds of UK aid to African agriculture and rural development goes on roads, paper and rubber schemes and a further 10% to support sugar, coffee, cocoa and tea developments. This compares with just 1.5% for the livestock sector and 1% for rural water supplies.

Commercial criteria, says the report, draw aid away from rural development to prestigious urban schemes. Hence the largest slice of UK aid to Sudan in recent years (£74 million) went to the building of Khartoum power station.

Research

Some major advances have been made in recent years, with British scientific contributions, in improving crops for suitable for drought prone areas. But the UK aid funding for this work has slipped backwards. The ODA funded Tropical Development and Research Institute has had its budget slashed in recent years and funding for important international research institutes has stagnated at a low level (£4.5 million in 1984).[29] Oxfam's representative in Ethiopia points out that, *"the Addis Ababa-based International Livestock Centre for Africa only receives £220,000 UK aid and ironically contributes more than this to Britain in goods and services bought here"*.

A team of scientists at Kew Gardens set up a 'Survey of Economic Plants for Arid and Semi-Arid Tropics' to develop improved varieties of traditional staple foods consumed in drought prone regions. One of the plants the team is working on is nicknamed 'green glue' which, say the scientists, could help reclaim deserts. The plants grow close to the ground in arid wastes and bind shifting desert sand together to reform soil. *"What is needed now"*, says the Kew Chief Scientist, Mr. Lucas, *"are field trials with backing from governments"*. Initially they were promised government funding, but later this decision was reversed. Rather than see the programme collapse, Oxfam has stepped in with funding.

Similarly, at the height of the Ethiopian famine, Oxfam made a grant to Wye College to safeguard continuing research on *t'eff*, a staple food in Ethiopia.

In 1984 the ODA supported only one research project on millet — the staple food of millions of the poor in many parts of Africa. The ODA provided £14,000. Twice this amount was spent on tobacco research.[30]

The government has made a number of statements recently about the importance of scientific research in combating famine, and some new grants have been made. Whether this represents a lasting change in aid priority remains to be seen. To be effective increased support should be in the form of local costs for overseas based research centres, and for employing local staff. The research undertaken should be determined after careful consultation with the communities involved.

Aid via the World Bank

The World Bank is the world's largest funding source for agricultural development. Britain provides about 8% of these funds, and has considerable influence within the World Bank. The EEC countries as a bloc have a voting power exceeding that of the USA.

The World Bank is often accused of favouring large-scale development schemes which are not in the best interests of the poor. Since 1974 only 16% of World Bank agricultural aid to sub-Saharan Africa was spent on rain-fed cereal growing, though the majority of Africa's farmers have no access to irrigation.[31]

In its recent report 'Poverty and Hunger', however, the World Bank has indicated that it may have been wrong in the past.[32] It has made similar statements before, but in recent years it had rather turned its back on the 'poverty focus'. This new policy is encouraging, but it remains to be seen how effectively it is implemented.

Other ways of helping the poor

Agricultural development relevant to the poor farmer in vulnerable areas is now widely argued to be a major priority for aid. Although it is important, it can only be one strand of an effective attack on poverty and hunger. Not all the hungry are small farmers, nor live in famine prone areas. The majority of the poor in Latin America, for instance, live in urban shanty towns. And in countries such as India and Bangladesh most of the rural poor either have too little land or are landless labourers who will not necessarily benefit from improvements in farming. In Africa, too, agricultural development by itself won't cure the problem of hunger, disease and poverty. Other ingredients are vital too, including environmental protection, creating jobs in both the cities and the rural areas, bringing safe water supplies to the poor, improving education and health services, health and nutrition education and welfare schemes such as low-price food distribution at times of severe hardship.

One way of reaching the poor is through special credit schemes or community banks. Poor people are often unable to get bank loans because they can offer no land or assets as security — especially in the case of women — and they may also be hampered by illiteracy. They are just as likely to have ideas for improving their income as wealthier people, but usually cannot borrow the money required by these schemes, or can only do so from a money-lender.

In Bangladesh local Oxfam staff report that traditional money-lenders frequently charge interest rates of 10–20% a *month*. Oxfam is funding many village banks, and providing the necessary credit for a range of initiatives, from making fishing nets to duck rearing. These schemes often have separate channels for lending to women to help them overcome the traditional difficulties they face in obtaining credit as well as giving them greater independence and control over their income.

Official aid can be used in a similar way. The Grameen Bank in Bangladesh —

supported by the International Fund for Agricultural Development, a multilateral aid agency — has a good record of providing credit to landlesss men and women.

Pitfalls

Aid that may be intended to help the poor by helping the economy of their country to grow, or even aid that is intended to benefit the poor directly, can end up causing hardship and poverty for many.

The World Bank, for example, is funding a number of schemes in remoter parts of Brazil which are intended to improve the country's economy, offer thousands of jobs, produce cheap power and improve communications. All of these objectives may be achieved, but the native people of those regions will suffer loss of livelihood and destruction of their environment.

In the tribal belt of Gujarat state, India, many families effectively lose their land when they need to borrow. The money-lenders insist on taking over the use of their farms as interest. One man, Kalvara, from Vangad village, had borrowed money for drugs to combat a creeping paralysis following a bout of malaria. The drugs didn't work, leaving Kalvara destitute and crippled. Many others in the same area had also lost the use of their land. Oxfam lent the capital needed to start a 'village bank' in the area, which quickly replaced the traditional money-lender. Kalvara and others borrowed from the bank at very low interest, paid off the money lenders and regained their land. Others in the village helped farm Kalvara's land while the use of his legs slowly returned. Now he is back on his feet again.

The 'Nordestão' scheme, for example, embraces a number of hydro-electric projects which, as Oxfam field staff argue, will have, *"serious implications for rural populations occupying lands to be flooded"*.[33] The 'Polonoroeste' project — a major road building and land development scheme — is opening up part of the Amazon region of Brazil to large ranch and estate owners. But it is clearing out the forest dwellers in the process.

In other parts of the world Oxfam staff tell similar stories.

The World Bank funded Narmada dam project in Gujarat, India, will displace tens of thousands of families living in the valley to be flooded. At the time of writing a question mark hangs over their future. Promises have been made to resettle them properly, but the first to be moved have received virtually no help. A compensation agreement has been reached between the Indian authorities and the World Bank, but it remains to be seen how this will be applied in practice.

The World Bank-funded Narmada Dam project in India will displace tens of thousands of people living in the valley to be flooded.

The ODA-funded Social Forestry scheme in Karnataka, India, was intended to benefit the poor by planting trees for fuel-wood and animal fodder. In some areas it is welcomed by poor, landless women, but in others the scheme has concentrated on trees such as eucalyptus that provide pulp for Mysore paper mills, but which, the local poor argue, do not provide the fuel-wood or animal fodder they need.

An ODA-funded scheme in Cajamarca, Peru, helped a major multinational food corporation introduce dairy farming. The scheme provided loans and veterinary services which encouraged small farmers to invest in dairy cows. The company was the sole purchaser of the milk produced and deducted loan instalments from the payments to farmers. The price of milk fell steeply and the poor have found themselves in a poverty trap. They can't sell their cows and return to shepherding because there's no market for dairy cows. But there's no future in producing milk either.

A way for aid

Aid projects intended to help the poor often go wrong. Sometimes wages don't arrive for the local staff. Sometimes there is corruption. Sometimes the design of the project is inappropriate and all to often failure stems from not involving the local people from the start in the very programme that is intended to help them.

Despite these difficulties, it is essential to continue to find ways to tackle poverty. At least mistakes can be rectified and lessons learned for the future. But to concentrate aid on power stations, helicopters or holiday villages because economists and planners are confident they will bring good financial returns is to turn our backs on the one priority voters and taxpayers want to see dominate the use of official aid — fighting poverty directly.

There are many illustrations of the damage that can be done in the name of compassion. To some people these examples are enough to conclude that official aid does more harm than good. This is a very pessimistic view. It is important to look at the successes and the failures of official aid, and from these to establish future priorities for aid use, based on the principle that the fundamental purpose of aid is the direct relief of poverty.

The goals

To respond to clear public concern by developing an aid programme that reflects in its scale and nature a sincere government commitment to the fight against poverty and hunger in the world. To assert that this is the principal objective of aid and far outweighs British commercial self-interest in its allocation. To demonstrate an intent to direct a much greater proportion of aid to the immediate needs of the poor.

Priorities for the British Government

1. To reduce the emphasis on commercial criteria in the allocation of aid. In particular, the commercial extreme of the aid programme — the Aid Trade Provision — should be phased out of the aid budget altogether and transferred to the Department of Trade and Industry, since its primary purpose is to win export contracts for UK firms.

2. To allocate aid where it will help the poor most effectively.

Which people: the 'Third World poor' do not form a homogeneous group. Some are peasant farmers who might benefit from agricultural development. Others are nomads who are threatened by the degradation of the environment. Some live in shanty towns and need improved health care and other basic services, while others face immediate starvation and need emergency relief. A different aid approach is needed for each group.

Which countries: the majority of the world's poorest people live in the poorest countries, and this should be reflected in the distribution of official aid. But many very poor people live in the slightly wealthier countries, and they should be helped too.

Which governments: some governments make it much easier than others to help their poor. Since aid in these countries can be particularly effective, it is important to give them special weight in the allocation of aid. In countries where the government is not concerned about fighting poverty, the only effective way of reaching the poor may be through voluntary agencies.

3. To involve the poor. To ensure that development schemes are long-lasting and that their benefits really do reach poor people, it is important that they respond to needs identified by the poor themselves. Great stress should be placed on 'popular participation' — involving poor communities in the design and execution of development projects — and in particular on the involvement of women, with special schemes to respond to their needs. All this necessitates forging a new 'partnership for development' with the governments of developing countries and, where this is not possible, channelling aid through voluntary agencies.

4. To increase the emphasis on agricultural development, rural development and aid specifically directed at poor people, particularly in the famine vulnerable areas, including:

a) Improving extension services (technical advice, veterinary services etc.) and particularly targeting them to women, so that poor farmers have access to improved methods.

b) Concentrating on agricultural schemes designed to improve the ability of those most at risk from hunger or famine to buy or grow the food for their family's basic needs.

c) Improving the rural infrastructure in the most vulnerable areas, including roads, rail, telephone systems and the supply of seeds, fertilisers and other inputs, when it is clear that these initiatives respond to the expressed needs of the poorest people.

d) Improving the prices paid directly to poor farmers for their produce.

e) Increasing and diversifying rural credit, so that small-scale farmers, men and women, are able to borrow what they need for seeds, irrigation systems, fertilisers etc.

f) Providing more support for UK, Third World-based and international institutes for research into food crops suitable for agriculturally vulnerable areas.

g) Supporting governments that are attempting to promote land reform.

5. To reform EEC food aid. Present procedures should be overhauled to increase the proportion available for famine relief (if the need arises), to phase out products such as milk powder and butter that are not basic foods, to phase out food aid schemes which conflict with the interests of local farmers and to concentrate non-emergency food aid on countries which both (a) *need* to import food and (b) are embarking on 'food strategies' designed to increase food production and deliver the benefits to the whole population.

6. To strengthen the EEC's capacity to respond to emergencies. This particularly involves reforming emergency food aid procedures. These reforms would include:

a) Improving early warning systems for the detection of famines at their earliest possible stage (and greater preparedness to respond to the alarms).

b) Setting up strategic emergency food reserves in famine-vulnerable countries, including help to cover the running costs.

c) Instituting swifter procedures for allocating emergency food aid.

d) An agreement to supplement the UK aid budget out of central government reserves in the event of major emergencies, such as the recent famine in Africa.

7. To make a full commitment to Unicef's 'Within Human Reach' strategy, in particular placing great stress on food security and on strengthening health, rural water supplies, education and other basic services needed by the poor.

8. To increase the emphasis on soil and water conservation, sand dune stabilisation, reafforestation and other measures to protect the environment and develop natural resources.

9. To argue in the international arenas for these 'Real Aid' criteria to be adopted by official aid agencies, especially by the multilateral agencies such as the World Bank.

10. To agree a five year timetable for reaching the UN target of 0.7% GNP as aid, concentrating the increase in the aid budget on the poverty-relieving programmes described above and on similar programmes of multilateral agencies.

TRADE

The Treadmill

One of the harshest realities of modern times is the vicious treadmill of the commodity trade. People in the rich world are proud of all the aid they and their governments gave for famine relief in Africa (three and a half billion dollars worth in 1985). And, true, the suffering would have been imponderably worse if that aid hadn't been given. But this must be put into perspective.

If Africa's trade hadn't collapsed, then the continent would have EARNED $5 billion extra in that year.

No-one is suggesting that all these extra earnings would have gone entirely to the drought regions and eradicated famine, but it would certainly have lessened the crisis. Countries on a sounder economic footing may have serious droughts, but they are likely to avoid catastrophic famines. Hence Kenya, which is wealthier because of its relatively advanced and diverse trade base, suffered a bad drought and harvest loss in many parts of the country in 1984, but avoided widespread famine.[1] Other countries, such as Mali or Burkina Faso, which are financially unhealthier, were simply unable to cope with their drought. In 1983, before the worst period of drought, Sudan's financial reserves had, for example, fallen to such a point that they only covered six days' worth of imports.[2] There's no safety margin in such an economic climate.

An understanding of hunger must encompass an understanding of the trade treadmill.

How the treadmill works

Step 1 — Need to earn more

If your rent goes up and the family food bill shoots up, you've got to earn more. That has been the problem of most developing countries over the first half of the 1980s. With rising interest rates and soaring prices of machinery, oil and other import needs, developing countries needed to earn more.

Step 2 — Limited opportunities

There are few ways in which developing countries can earn more. Three quarters of their earnings come from just 33 key commodities and an individual country is likely to be heavily dependent on just one or two of these.[3] The markets for these commodities are limited.

For example, in 1984 88% of Zambia's export earnings came from copper,

50% of Sudan's from cotton, 51% of Malawi's from tobacco and 59% of Bangladesh's from jute.[4] Most of the commodities are agricultural products, but some countries depend on mineral exports.

The Third World's dependence on a handful of raw commodities comes from necessity rather than choice. They need to earn foreign exchange, and virtually all other ways of doing so are denied them. They would like to sell other goods — process their commodities and produce manufactured goods — but the wealthy countries, their would-be customers, erect barriers to such trade.

Step 3 — Facing competition

Commodity prices tumble as developing countries produce more for export and compete with each other to find outlets for their goods. This problem has been sharpened by the recession faced by industrialised countries, which meant they were cutting imports, and by the development of synthetics to replace natural

Case Study — Brazil

The effect of the trade treadmill can be seen in the case of Brazil. Throughout the country the export drive is indicating how land is used. Brazil is now one of the world's leading food exporters, yet millions of its people are malnourished. To pay for the interest on its $100,000 million debts, and to meet the capital repayments due, Brazil has had to go hell-for-leather for export growth. The growth has been remarkable. Brazil now has a $12,400 million trade surplus — more than enough to service its debts.[8] The acreage under soya bean has increased more than twenty-fold from 1963–83, overtaking all other crops except maize.[9] Most soya is exported as animal food and by 1983 accounted for about 10% of Brazil's foreign exchange.

Oranges are Brazil's latest boom crop. Production has increased two and a half times over the last ten years and Brazil is now the world's leading producer of orange juice.[10]

The Brazilian sugar trade has not been so lucrative. Production has soared, but exports have to be subsidised — such is the eagerness for foreign exchange to pay their import bills. The main use of the increased sugar production, however, is to ferment into alcohol which, in the 'Gasahol' programme, is used to replace petrol in cars.

Oxfam staff report the clearing of peasants from land which has been taken over for cocoa production in north east Brazil. This process has been gradual and steady over many years. In the state of Bahia as a whole, the number of cocoa trees has increased by 40% in ten years. Oxfam is supporting legal costs of lawyers who are representing hundreds of families in their cases against the encroaching landlords.

The pressure on land in the Amazon region is even more dramatic. In products such as cotton and jute. Increased production in a declining market results in commodity prices falling even lower.

Step 4 — Running faster

To maintain constant export earnings means selling even larger quantities. For many countries this means using more and more of the best quality land to grow for export.

Step 5 — Back to the beginning

The more that is exported, the faster prices fall. This spiral led to a full 18% fall in the price index for primary commodities in the first five years of this decade.[5] The loss in earnings for the Third World of about $40 billion per year is much more than the aid those countries receive.[6] This comes at a time when prices of the goods they import are higher and the debt repayment is most severe.

the state of Acre in Brazil's western corner the local people collect rubber and gather Brazil nuts for their livelihood. They live in ecological harmony with the rain forests. However, this is changing rapidly, as wealthy ranchers from the South and multinational companies move in. After clearing the forests there is a great deal of profit to be made in beef ranching, selling the meat for export. Cattle meat exports have expanded seven times in ten years.

The juggernaut of progress seems unstoppable. The rubber tappers have tried to defend their forests and their traditional way of life, but it is particularly difficult, as they are scattered in isolated communities. They decided that the only hope was to band together with rubber tappers from other parts of the Amazon. Helped by funding from Oxfam, 120 people from different areas came together for the first ever national meetings of rubber tappers in October 1985 in the capital city, Brasilia. For some the journey was immense. One woman travelled for 13 days by canoe and then seven days in buses and boats to take part. The meeting was not just a chance to exchange experiences and plans. It also enabled the rubber tappers to meet with government representatives and to explain their problems directly.

The contrasts between a country which is one of the world's leading food exporters, and yet in which many people are malnourished is a harsh reality indeed. But the answer to Brazil's crisis of hunger doesn't simply hinge on what crops are grown. The pivotal issues are how wealth and power are shared within that country, and the external economic pressures created by the debt crisis and world recession.

Indexes of real commodity prices, 1965–84

Index (1980 = 100)

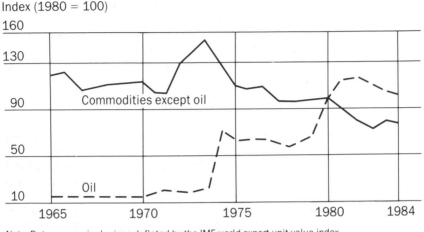

Note: Data are nominal prices deflated by the IMF world export unit value index.
Source: World Bank data.

For Africa the situation is particularly grim. The terms of trade — the ratio between prices it pays for imports and receives for its exports — are worse than at any time in the past 30 years.[7] This is the treadmill: racing faster and faster, not even to stand still, but to move inexorably backward.

Who are the losers?

The land used by developing countries to grow the major export crops increased 11% from 1974 to 1984.[11] Since most of this was better quality land, peasant farmers have been forced increasingly onto less productive areas.

In a similar period (between 1973 and 1983) the area under cereals and root crops in poor countries increased by some 8%. The area under soya beans, coffee and sugar grew particularly fast in this period, increasing by 48%.[12]

From 1975 to 1980 developing countries increased their volume of non-oil exports by 9.4%.[13] This is not, in itself, a problem. Most people in Britain drink tea, eat rice, use rubber tyres, wear cotton shirts and many smoke cigarettes. If a developing country has a particularly good climate and soil for growing coffee, for example, it seems to make good financial sense to use the land to grow coffee for export, and to import food with the earnings. Developing countries, say economists, have 'comparative advantage' in the production of tropical products because of their favourable agricultural conditions. But the trade treadmill doesn't allow this to happen. The race to export is fuelled by a need for foreign exchange — dollars that are needed to pay interest charges and soaring import bills.

While over-production for export without a matching increase in demand results in falling prices for commodities, if farmers neglect food production then the prices of local foodstuffs wil soar. The middle class and wealthy grumble, but pay the higher bills. The poor simply can't afford to. For the governments, it's easier to keep their own hungry people at bay than foreign creditors. More and more people go hungry, and are forced to eat weeds, roots and other forest produce — sometimes food they know is poisonous — in order to live from day to day. For the poor, 'comparative advantage' becomes 'absolute disadvantage'.

Many countries suffer the 'absolute disadvantage'.

Tanzania

The amount of coffee Tanzania had to export to pay for a ten ton truck doubled from 1960 to 1970, and doubled again in the seventies. Tanzania greatly increased its coffee production in the 1970s, but with falling coffee prices and rising prices of oil and manufactured goods, the increased coffee harvest was worth less than at the start of the decade.[14]

1982 to 1985 saw an increase in the price of coffee — to the extent that economists predicted that this crop offered a breakthrough for African countries facing economic difficulties. Then came the collapse. In January 1986 coffee fetched $2.20 per pound. By July it had tumbled to $1.37 — just two fifths of the price it had been in 1975.

Bangladesh

Oxfam staff in Bangladesh describe how, following a period of reasonable prices, poor farmers put over their land to growing jute. By 1986 the price had collapsed and these farmers were having to sell their jute below the cost of growing it.

Burkina Faso

Cotton output in this West African country shot up 37 times to 75,000 tons from 1960 to 1984.[15] At the same time the production of millet and sorghum (staple foods of the poor) barely doubled.

Mali

Cotton production also increased eight-fold in Mali over the last 20 years, while food production has declined 10%.[16] A recent report from Oxfam's Country Representative tells how world cotton prices nosedived just as Mali gathered a record harvest. The loss to the national treasury is estimated to be $30 million, a seventh of its entire budget.[17]

Kenya

According to World Bank estimates, Kenya has one of the highest rates of malnutrition in the world, yet some of its best agricultural land is used for export crops.[18] For instance a Brooke Bond subsidiary grows carnations and other flowers on land by the side of Lake Naivasha. The flowers are then rushed in refrigerated trucks to Nairobi airport and flown to the UK. Estate owners earn much more by growing flowers for European buttonholes than food for Kenyan people.

Niger

It is not just agricultural commodities that have taken a knock. In 1982 uranium accounted for 80% of Niger's export earnings. The recent price collapse of uranium ore, has, therefore, had a devastating effect on the country's economy. In just one year Niger has seen 27% wiped off the value of its total exports.[19]

Indonesia

The fall in the price of oil has hit some of the poorer oil producers badly. Indonesia has had to cut its development budget by 22%. *"The government has been trying to promote rapid expansion in rubber, palm oil, tea and coffee production to compensate for its loss of oil revenue"*, comments Oxfam's Country Representative. Exports are growing rapidly, but the average yield for these crops has been declining, in part because the crop expansion means moving into marginal lands. A new, ambitious programme is now under way to grow cotton in some of the smaller eastern islands.

Meanwhile the government has made great efforts to increase rice production, and is now almost self-sufficient, but a consequence has been the decline or stagnation of other crops needed for a balanced diet.

The role of governments

The trade treadmill also encourages governments to focus on using the most fertile land to help the national economy, rather than for growing food for their population.

In Ethiopia most of the government's agricultural budget has been used to increase the production for export of coffee and other crops in the state farms, notably in the Awash valley, while relatively little has been done for the pastoralists or small farmers in the drought regions of Wollo and Tigre. In Sudan the major investment is in the eastern area of Gezira, described by and ex-Oxfam Field Secretary for the region as *"one large government farm."*

Too much

Sometimes a consequence of the export drive is to produce more crops than can possibly be sold. In Europe, the African famine drew public attention to the tragedy of famine in one part of the world co-existing with mountains of surplus in another. But the deeper irony is that some of the worst affected countries were building up their own surpluses as the famine unfolded. Sudan's cotton stock expanded to 550,000 bales — worth over $500 million.[20] There is so much cotton on the world market that it is almost impossible to sell. As with Europe's well publicised butter deals, Sudan is now subsidising cotton sales to the Eastern bloc countries on barter trade deals.

In 1985, famine-stricken Sudan had a huge stockpile of cotton — virtually unsaleable because of a world market glut.

Ethiopia also has too much. In this case it is coffee stocks which are piling up. There was a surplus of 2.6 million bags at the beginning of the 1984/85 season, down to 2.1 million at the outset of the 1985/86 season.[21]

Selling the future

The seeds of despair for generations to come are being sown by the hasty stripping of natural resources for short term economic reasons. At current logging rates, the jungles of South East Asia, which supply over three quarters of the world's tropical hardwood exports, will completely disappear within 50 years.[22] An irreplaceable resource which took millions of years to evolve — gone in a generation. The Food and Agriculture Organisation (FAO) has warned that forest land elsewhere is under grave threat, that a fifth of the world's forests will be destroyed or severely depleted within 15 years. Raising cattle for export, states the FAO, is the chief culprit in Latin America.

In Bangladesh there is a different, more bizarre environmental problem: Europe's taste for frogs legs. Oxfam's Representative in Bangladesh describes widespread anxiety that this new and rapidly increasing export line, supported by EEC aid, is not only cruel, but also damaging to the environment. The frogs are not specially bred but captured in the wild. In their natural habitat they eat the insects that attack the crops. Already their population is depleted and crop loss is increasing substantially in some areas.

The growers' reward

With export crops, not only are the world prices at rock bottom level, but only a meagre proportion of the price reaches the poor who grow them.

In Uganda, for example, coffee tends to be grown by small farmers. This is one of the few crops they can grow and be confident they'll be able to sell for ready cash. But in 1984 the Ugandan peasant only received 19% of the world market price for coffee received by the Ugandan government.[23] (The situation has improved recently and the government has undertaken to give growers half the proceeds).

Coffee growers receive a small proportion of the price in the Dominican Republic, too. As the economic situation worsens, the power of the middle-men has increased. Oxfam has funded a small network of groups to help producers break into direct exporting, by-passing the middle-men and so earning considerably more.[24]

A recent Oxfam report describes how, in Sudan, the government fixed price for gum arabic, which was a major export product and a precious resource, is so low that peasant collectors have now turned to burning their trees. They can earn more by selling charcoal than gum arabic.[25]

Protection — the rich countries' rules

The 50 poorest countries could double their export earnings if they could process their commodities and export cocoa powder rather than beans, instant coffee rather than coffee beans for example.[26] They do try to break into these markets, but find that the industrialised countries impose tariffs on such imports, restrict access by rigid quotas or impose other barriers. Nearly a third of developing countries' agricultural exports to the West are restricted by such barriers. For cocoa, coffee, rubber and tobacco only a fifth (in terms of value) was imported in processed form by developed countries.[27]

There is even fiercer protection when it comes to manufactured goods. Only 3% of manufactured goods sold in industrialised countries are made in developing countries.[28] The trade in textiles — fibres, fabrics and clothes — is the classic example. Eighty percent of this $100 billion a year trade is covered by the Multifibre Arrangement (MFA), a system of import barriers that protects the domestic textile industries of the rich countries.[29] It is understandable that governments are concerned to protect jobs and investment at home, but the traditional textile industry is declining anyway as synthetics and highly automated production methods are being developed. Both Labour and Conservative administrations, and industry and Trade Unions in Britain have supported the MFA, but there is an emerging consensus that it needs softening, especially in respect of the poor countries. Britain has given some countries a 'most favoured nation' status. Ironically this list includes none of the poorer countries, but does include South Africa, the USA and Japan.[30] It is imports from the wealthier textile producing countries, not imports from the Third World, that threaten jobs, and yet the MFA hits Third World countries the hardest.

Bangladesh, for example, has tried to export shirts to the UK, but import restrictions were imposed even before it had a chance to corner more than a tiny share of the market. After intense public lobbying of Parliament, the government announced in July 1986 that the UK quota restriction for Bangladesh shirts would be lifted until at least 1991.

The British Prime Minister, Margaret Thatcher, replying to an Oxfam supporter who had lobbied her on this and other issues, said that she fully recognised *"that one of the most effective ways open to us to help the poorest countries is to provide a secure market for their goods, so that they can build up new industries with confidence".*[31] She recognised the special circumstances of countries like Bangladesh and their dependence on textiles, as did other EEC governments, and consequently the European Commission has been mandated to negotiate more liberal treatment for the poorest countries in the new MFA. It remains to be seen if the new terms go anywhere near far enough.

Compounding the problem

A number of factors make the trade treadmill more treacherous.

Western aid

Most Western aid for agriculture supports the production of a few key export crops. Even in famine stricken Ethiopia, the majority of EEC agricultural aid has been for coffee production. Some economists have argued that this support for the export sector has helped bring world commodity prices down, and so gives more benefits to the donors than to the developing countries.[32]

Speculation

Improving commodity prices is easier said than done. The market is determined by the buyer, not the seller, and indeed the major auction rooms where prices are determined — the Commodity Exchanges — are in New York, London and other Western cities. There may be scores of countries trying to sell their produce which have just one thing in common — a need for foreign exchange. A handful of buyers — notably the transnational corporations — control the lion's share of world trade in tea, coffee, cocoa, sugar, edible oils, tobacco and other commodities. Many of the buyers are simply speculators, who may 'sell' goods before they have 'bought' them, or buy warehouses full of commodities and sell again hours later without any suggestion that the goods might actually be moved. Speculators don't care if the prices of commodities go up or down as long as they can predict a trend and make a fast buck. Such is the magnitude of this commodities roulette, it is estimated that only 5% of commodity deals relate to the delivery of actual goods. Speculation on this scale grossly exaggerates the free market trends. A whisper of a frost in Brazil sends coffee prices rocketing and the hint that the US is to sell some of its stockpiled copper sends all the metal markets into a deep descending spiral.

The monopoly of transnational companies

While the Commodity Exchanges are bad news for developing countries, the major companies are often able to go a step further. They can bypass the auction rooms altogether and do a deal with a Third World government for virtually the whole of that country's production of a commodity.

A rare insight into commodity trading was given by Nestlé — the world's largest trader of coffee, cocoa and milk. In its 1976 report 'Nestlé in Developing Countries', the company stated: *"the volume of our purchases of coffee and cocoa is so vast that it influences the market for these commodities"*. Susan George, academic and author of many books on development issues, has compared information in this report with that published elsewhere and discovered, for example, that in 1974 Nestlé paid the Ivory Coast just a quarter of the average world price for coffee and Ghana half the going rate for cocoa.[33] Similarly, Del Monte has a long-standing agreement with the Kenyan government giving it a monopoly over the pineapple trade. This agreement has helped Del Monte corner a large proportion of the world market in this fruit.

The companies involved in commodity trade, shipping, wholesaling and retailing, take the major share of the final selling price for Third World produce. It is estimated that only 11.5% of the retail price of bananas — a commodity which, after all, requires little processing — gets back to the producer countries. With tea it is not more than 30%.[34]

The major companies probably have greater influence over world trade than governments. They control, after all, 40% of the entire world's trade and up to 90% of commodity trade.[35] The top 30 companies on average each had a bigger trade than the exports of the poorest 50 countries put together.[36] Any bid to give developing countries a better deal in commodity trading must, therefore, consider carefully the role of the transnationals.

The need for alternatives

Some people argue that developing countries should simply pull out of world trade and 'go it alone', moving away from a trade system based on money and reducing imports. These may be temporary solutions for some developing countries, but more permanent measures are needed for a global trading strategy. A fair and reliable trading regime for commodities demands stability of price and supply. Developing countries also need the opportunities to earn more by exporting processed commodities. This means dismantling the trade barriers erected by Western countries.

To do so may also be in Western interests. Certainly there are short term benefits from cheap commodity prices: Victor Keegan of *The Guardian* has argued that the main reason that Britain enjoys a falling rate of inflation is

44

because world commodity prices fell 20% in sterling terms over 1985.[37] But will these benefits last? The FAO has warned that falling commodity prices and increased protectionism by the rich countries have brought the world to the brink of a trade war in which no-one will benefit.[38]

So what alternatives are there?

The ways forward

An alternative system of trade giving better prices for commodities could emerge through co-operation between developing countries, the effective working of international commodity agreements, the imposition of codes of conduct on transnational corporations and the development of effective insurance schemes to compensate developing countries when their export earnings fall.

Banding together

By close co-operation, developing countries have the power to improve their terms of trade, both in what they sell and in what they buy.

Producer cartels — where countries exporting a common commodity agree amongst themselves a minimum selling price — are a starting point. The oil producers' cartel, OPEC, is the obvious example. Less well-known, but also effective, has been the cartel of diamond producers which, curiously, had the leading diamond company, De Beers, as an honorary member. Evidence shows that cartels work when the buyers cannot do without the product, and when if it is not sold, it is left unexploited. For perishable goods, however, or for commodities that have been stockpiled by the major buyers, a cartel would have limited power.

Many developing countries are beginning to break out of the 'North–South' pattern and are buying goods that they need from each other, in exchange for goods they produce. For example Nigeria swaps crude oil for Brazilian-made Volkswagen kits. It is estimated that 15–30% of world trade is now in this 'barter-trade' form.

To strengthen this 'South-South' trade, groups of countries have formed their own regional trading arrangements, such as the Latin American Free Trade Association, the Association of South East Asian Nations, the Economic Commission of West African States and the Preferential Trade Agreement of South and East Africa. One trading group — the Andean Pact — has very much strengthened trade and other forms of co-operation within Latin America. For example, rather than each country individually setting up a fertiliser plant, they have jointly set up their own agricultural chemicals industry.

A new form of co-operation which is as yet in its early days is joint *importing* arrangements. By joining forces and buying together the goods needed from industrialised countries, developing countries may be able to shave 5% off import bills.[39] This could save $20–25 billion per year, almost as much as they receive in aid.

Codes of conduct for transnational corporations (TNCs)

The need for internationally agreed rules to govern the operations of transnational corporations is a subject of intense discussion. A special unit — the UN Centre for Transnational Corporations (UNCTC) — was set up in 1979 as a result. Its director, Peter Hanson, has suggested that an international Code of Conduct may be agreed under UN auspices by the end of 1987.[40] The difficulty with codes of conduct is that they tend to be unenforceable and too general, so they may do more harm than good by allowing 'business as normal' under a veneer of control.

One major stumbling block faced by the proposed UNCTC code involves transfer pricing — the selling of produce at artificial prices from one subsidiary company to another in order to transfer profits to the parent company's home country or to a tax haven. It is estimated that inter-firm trade of this nature within transnational corporations accounts for between 25% and 50% of all world trade. Other contentious areas in the drafting of the code are corporate responsibility for environmental protection, industrial relations principles and compensation paid in the event of nationalisation.

As many TNCs are US-based, it seems extremely unlikely that the US government will cooperate with the UNCTC code. USSR support may also be withheld if there is general agreement that Soviet enterprises operating abroad count as transnationals.

Whether or not a generalised code for TNCs will ever be agreed and operate effectively remains to be seen. Experience to date shows that effective international measures can be agreed on very specific issues such as the marketing of baby milk, pharmaceuticals or pesticides, but that even these are highly complex and depend on the companies' voluntary compliance (albeit under strong moral international pressure). An overall code for TNCs will have to be supplemented by a framework of controls for specific business activities.

Commodity agreements

There have been a number of attempts to improve and stabilise commodity prices through international agreements between the major producer and consumer countries. Some may have been more successful than others. So far they have covered seven commodities: copper, wheat, tin, cocoa, sugar, rubber and coffee. The International Coffee Agreement (ICA), now 24 years old, has been more successful than the others — certainly in terms of stabilising prices — but even this has nonetheless faced great difficulties.

In some commodity agreements, the producers and consumers fix quotas for the amount that each country can export. They may also buy in buffer stocks of the commodity if the world price falls below a certain level. Conversely, if the price goes above another trigger level, the buffer stocks are sold off.

There is general pessimism today about the effectiveness of buffer stocks, however. They are extremely expensive to maintain and generally have the effect of keeping prices down rather than up. And without almost unlimited financial resources the commodity agreements collapse when there is a major drop in the market for that commodity. This was demonstrated by the collapse in October 1985 of the International Tin Council. The dramatic fall in the price of tin that ensued has plunged the economy of Bolivia (40% of whose exports derive from tin) into chaos. Families in the mining belt face extreme poverty and malnutrition has increased as a result. Oxfam has recently given a grant to a group of mining families to help them set up a food buying co-operative — buying in bulk in order to get basic food at cheaper prices.

The Common Fund

In 1976 the UN Conference on Trade and Development (UNCTAD) proposed the setting up of an Integrated Programme for Commodities (IPC) to give protection for 18 key commodities comprising 87% of the Third World's non-oil commodity exports.[41] The IPC involves setting up a 'Common Fund' which would be used to finance buffer stocks, and would also help developing countries increase their processing of commodities — probably a more important contribution.

The Common Fund does not yet exist. It is supported by the British government, but to have a chance of getting off the ground it needs the backing of either the US or the USSR. At present this looks unlikely since, as producers of raw commodities themselves, this initiative would not necessarily be in their own interests.

Price insurance schemes

Two schemes exist which are intended to stabilise commodity earnings.

The first is the Compensatory Finance Facility (CFF) of the IMF. In theory IMF member countries are automatically allowed to borrow funds on a short term basis if their export earnings fall. Since 1981, however, the IMF has imposed similar austerity conditions on the CFF as for normal IMF loans.

Secondly, the EEC has its own schemes, funded by its aid budget, under the Lomé convention. These cover agricultural commodities (the STABEX scheme) and minerals (SYSMIN). The schemes are restricted, however, to the African, Caribbean and Pacific (ACP) countries with which the EEC has a special relationship, and they apply only to specified commodities. Sugar — produced of course in the EEC — is a notable omission from the list, and countries such as India and Bangladesh are excluded. Nevertheless the scheme is widely regarded as the best support yet for commodity producers. Under STABEX, developing countries get automatic loans (grants in the case of the poorest countries) if export earnings from the specified commodities fall. The main problem with the scheme is that there are insufficient funds to meet more than half the claims received, because the EEC continually fails to commit enough funds to ensure that it works efficiently.

Britain's role in fair trade

Britain is not only a major trading nation, it is also the home of many of the world's commodity exchanges and trade organisations. This gives it considerable power to change the rules of international trade — power that could and should be used to influence and develop trade patterns that are fairer for the Third World. Accepting 'fair trade' as a goal leads to a range of policy options that a British government could pursue for the benefit of the world's poor.

The goals

To improve the prices paid for the goods exported by developing countries; to allow those countries the chance to increase the range of goods they export and to develop stricter ethical standards in world trade. These measures by themselves may not benefit the poor directly but, for those governments with the political will to do so, they create the opportunity to tackle the underlying causes of their country's poverty.

Responsibility for achieving these goals also rests with the transnational corporations, with commodity speculators and with governments of developing countries and the Eastern bloc.

How the British government could help

1. Assist the co-operation between developing countries designed to improve their own trade opportunities. This could mean giving funding support to regional trade initiatives and financing research into the strengthening of trade between developing countries.

2. Reduce tariff and other barriers designed to protect the UK market from Third World imports, especially in the case of the poorest countries. In particular to phase out restrictions and tariffs on the import of processed commodities, to exempt the textile exports of the poorest countries from the restrictions of the Multifibre Arrangement and to allow a wider market access for manufactured goods from developing countries.

3. Support international efforts to impose controls on harmful business practices, in particular by:—

a) Introducing and enforcing codes of conduct in the trade of potentially hazardous or misused products (such as pesticides, chemicals, pharmaceuticals, baby milks).

b) Investigating and drawing up rules to curb speculation on the commodity markets and the export of profits from developing countries to tax havens.

4. Support efforts — such as those of the Common Fund and international commodity agreements — to improve the real price of commodities.

5. Call for increased funding and more flexible procedures to make existing export earnings compensation schemes work effectively. These include the Compensatory Finance Facility of the IMF and the EEC's STABEX scheme. The latter should be reformed and enlarged so that it covers all low income countries (not just the ACP states), and all commodities exported by developing countries, and it should receive adequate funds to respond to all applications.

Cane-growing countries like Jamaica suffer when EEC sugar surpluses depress the world market.

AGRICULTURE
The EEC Mountains

Introduction

Taxpayers in Europe, the US and Japan will pay out £27,000 million in direct subsidies for food production in 1986. This sum of money is more than three times the combined gross national product of Ethiopia and Sudan. The results will be vast surpluses in some countries and fatal shortages in others.

These contrasts were pointed out in April 1986, not by a stalwart of the development lobby, but by the Foreign Secretary, Sir Geoffrey Howe. Europe, he observed, was storing at public expense half a million tonnes of beef, 16 million tonnes of grain, a million tonnes of butter and enough wine to fill 64,000 Olympic-size swimming pools. Storage costs alone amount to £360 million per year.[1]

A cruel paradox highlighted by Sir Geoffrey is that too much food in some parts of the world aggravates shortages in the poorer countries. Food sold at subsidised prices on the world market depresses prices and makes Third World production uneconomic. That compounds the effects of droughts and other disasters.

The 'problem' of over-production isn't confined to Europe. The USA has an even bigger grain surplus — some 80 million tonnes — which is expected to double in 1987. The total bill for maintaining these surplus-producing policies is estimated at $100 billion per year.[2] For every $1 given as overseas aid, $3 are spent on the food mountains.

Another concerned critic of the Common Agricultural Policy is Sir Henry Plumb, ex-President of the National Farmers Union and leader of the Conservative group in the European Parliament. He told an audience at the Royal Show in July 1985 that the EEC's Common Agricultural Policy, *"has had a major impact on Third World agriculture. . . Countries which could grow more of the extra food they need are discouraged from doing so. The policy increases the variability of world market prices and increases uncertainty for importing and exporting countries alike, particularly the poorer countries. . . The net effect of the policy is lower food production in developing countries, greater uncertainty and inequitable, rigid trade flows. . . We are dumping food on world markets and creating artificially low prices".*[3]

These are harsh claims to be made about an agricultural policy covering a handful of countries in Europe. But the connection between Northern agriculture and Third World hunger was made frequently, in a different form,

Case Study — Ecuador

Ecuador's main export crop has traditionally been bananas. Now it is seeking to diversify. The banana market is relatively stable, but very little of the final retail price (only about 11p in the pound) gets back to the producer country. Ecuador is now trying to break into the palm oil market.

Forty thousand hectares of oil palm have been cultivated, producing 77,000 tonnes of oil per year and the plan is to increase the area ten times. British government aid, via the Commonwealth Development Corporation, is providing a loan of £6.5 million (15% of total costs) towards the scheme.

Oxfam's staff locally are concerned about the social and environmental consequences of this scheme. Forests are being cut down to make way for the new plantations, and this has already affected 10,000 of the indigenous people.

Besides causing the destruction of forests, palm oil processing produces wastes that cause serious pollution of the environment.

Oxfam has given a grant to the groups representing the Indians affected to help them in their campaign to draw attention to the social and environmental problems of the scheme.

Whether or not Ecuador as a country benefits from the plantations depends on the movements in the world vegetable oil trade, and the EEC's policies are of critical importance. With growing pressure to reduce surpluses and the cost of the CAP, the EEC is very likely to introduce incentives to farmers to move away from cereals into oilseed rape. This shift could dramatically reduce world prices and lead to an overproduction of vegetable oil.

Already there is something of a glut, and Malaysia now has a lake of palm oil it can't sell. Prices have fallen considerably — 50% between April and October 1985 — and Ecuador could end up destroying its forest and indigenous cultures to produce a product that nobody wants.

during the height of public concern over the famine in Africa. Then the contrast highlighted by the media was between the food aid needs of the starving and the mountains of surplus in Europe (enough grain to feed the 30 million famine victims of Africa for three years on refugee rations). Britain alone has £1400 million worth of food in its intervention stores.[4]

Clearly, the agricultural policies of North America and other non-EEC 'northern' countries also have considerable impact on the 'south', but Oxfam, as a British agency, is concerned to emphasise the role of the EEC. So can these surpluses both have contributed to hunger in the Third World *and* be used to relieve it? To answer this question it is necessary to understand how the EEC's agricultural policies work. Much of what follows is drawn from an Oxfam paper 'How Farming In Europe Affects the Third World Poor', which was produced as the background paper for a series of seminars involving members of the British farming community and Oxfam.[5]

How the CAP works

The Common Agricultural Policy was introduced in 1964 with the following aims:
■ to improve the stability of food supply
■ to increase self-sufficiency in food production
■ to maintain jobs on the land
■ to ensure a 'fair rate of return' for those who invested in land
■ to keep prices stable and reasonable for the consumer.
There are two main ways in which agriculture is supported:
1. Keeping up prices by:
a) **Target Prices** — fixing minimum prices — usually much higher than the world price — at which the EEC agencies guarantee to buy up farm produce. This encourages overproduction of the cereals, sugar, milk, meats and certain fruits and vegetables covered by this method.
b) **Production Aid** — where the farmer is paid the difference between the official support price and market price (used for tobacco, olive oil and pasta wheat).
2. Keeping competition out.
A complex system of levies and duties that protect the market from many imports. This creates an 'untree' market in which Third World countries cannot compete, even if — as is often the case — they can produce food more cheaply than EEC farmers.

Having generated overproduction, the EEC has four ways of dealing with the surpluses, and these also crucially affect the Third World. The surpluses can be:
■ put into intervention stores
■ dumped on the world market — i.e. sold at highly subsidised prices
■ given as food aid to developing countries
■ destroyed — or sold within the EEC at subsidised prices for non-food use.
Perishables such as fruits and vegetables are destroyed or converted into industrial alcohol, grain and milk are sold cheaply as animal food, and some grain is sold to the chemical industry.

Europe's food system and the Third World

The food Europe buys and sells has a powerful influence on the choice of crops grown in developing countries, on the prices that slum dwellers pay for their food and on the foreign exchange available to Third World governments.

There is a common assumption that the EEC, with all its surpluses and frequent talk of food aid to the hungry, must be a net supplier of food to the Third World. The reality is very different. The EEC imports £7 billion more from the developing world than it exports to it.[6] And that is before wood, rubber and cotton are included. For Britain this trade gap is £1.5 billion — more than the total UK aid.[7] But it is not only Europe that is dependent on imported food. The United States, generally regarded as the breadbasket of the world, is poised to become a net food importer for the first time since 1959. US food imports, mainly from Mexico, Brazil and Canada, are likely to amount to $24 billion in 1986 — slightly more than total food exports — while their grain mountains reach record heights.[8]

The EEC is the largest importer of agricultural products in the world and 60% of these come from the Third World. Some of the produce — such as tea, coffee, cocoa and rubber — cannot be grown in Europe. But others can — such as animal feed, vegetable oil, tobacco, cotton and sugar.

The EEC is also the second largest exporter of agricultural products in the world. The Third World is a major customer, notably for dairy products and cereals. Some EEC exports — notably sugar — compete heavily with Third World produce.

It is not easy to unravel the way in which Europe's food system affects the world's poor. Some people in the Third World undoubtedly benefit from the EEC's policies while others lose out.

There are three main issues, however; EEC exports, EEC imports and the EEC's effect on price stability. Each country is affected differently by the EEC, depending on what it produces.

All Third World countries, however, are affected by the destabilising influence the CAP has on world agricultural prices. Levies designed to bring the price of imports into line with prices within the Community stabilise prices in Europe, but at the expense of prices elsewhere. This uncertainty tends to encourage Third World producers — who can't afford to take risks — to shift to producing other crops with more stable prices.

Dumping of EEC surpluses on the world market also sends world prices plummeting with often disastrous consequences for Third World countries.

The CAP has caused the demand for some Third World produce to decline (notably sugar, beef, fruit and vegetables), while the demand for some produce has increased (such as manioc from Thailand for animal feed).

Overproduction resulting from the CAP has led to a drop in world cereal prices which, it could be argued, has helped developing countries who import basic foods. But this cheap food regime may encourage developing countries to switch from growing their own basic food to growing for export.[12] Since the CAP has greatly increased instability in world agricultural markets, it is quite likely that, in future, this switch will prove a costly mistake.

The development movement is faced with a dilemma. Should it argue for higher prices for Third World commodities and free access to European markets for goods from developing countries? Or should it encourage greater food self-sufficiency in Europe and less need for Third World imports?

Example of sugar

The EEC produces about a seventh of the world sugar crop, about three million tonnes per year more than it needs, because the CAP affords farmers very high prices for sugar beet.[10] Rather than build up another embarrassing mountain, the EEC exports vast quantities of sugar — the three million tonne surplus — usually at highly subsidised prices. The world market is consequently saturated and prices have fallen.

In the summer of 1985 world sugar prices crashed to below 2p per pound, compared with 7p per pound the previous June.[11] Prices have recovered considerably since then, but still only amount to about half the cost of production in most cane producing countries. Hence many Third World countries — who have depended on cane sugar production for generations — are having to sell at a loss. They continue to export sugar because they desperately need the foreign exchange and there are few alternatives.

The EEC does have a scheme to help sugar-producing countries — one of the very few examples in the world of an altruistic trade policy. Under the 'Sugar Protocol' the EEC imports some 1.3 million tonnes of sugar from certain developing countries at close to the EEC price. This arrangement arose from Britain's entry to the Common Market when Britain's commitment to poor Commonwealth cane producing countries was a major political issue.

Oxfam's work in a number of countries has been influenced by the difficulties faced by Third World sugar producers. For instance, the collapse of the sugar industry in the island of Negros in the Philippines has brought widespread unemployment and increased poverty.

Oxfam has provided grants to pay for feeding centres and to help the unemployed sugar workers to grow rice, maize and vegetables on the uncultivated sugar land.

The former would improve the prospects for Third World trade, but would encourage export crop production. The latter would worsen the terms of trade, but might encourage land use for growing locally needed food instead of exports. The answer to the dilemma lies in balance and stability. The EEC needs to work with the governments of developing countries to stabilise the supply of food needed by the poor, to make sure that food reaches the hungry and to safeguard the agriculture of developing countries from the instabilities caused by EEC policies.

Shared tasks of EEC and Third World governments

It is now generally agreed that the solution to hunger is not simply a technical one of growing more food. Social and political solutions are needed — ensuring that the poor are able to earn enough to buy the food they need or have land enough to grow for their needs.

In theory, increasing prices paid for Third World commodities and opening up the EEC market to imports allows a greater income earning ability for the Third World. In practice it can work the other way. Export crops can mean large mechanised plantations with very few people gaining employment, and those who do often being paid pitifully low wages. That is, however, an issue for Third World governments themselves to resolve. The EEC has relatively little influence. Aid programmes and agricultural advice from Europe have a bearing, but the distribution of land ownership, agricultural planning and terms of employment for farm labourers are political issues that can only be addressed by Third World governments. Europe can, however, give all the help possible to governments embarking on programmes of land reform, supporting agriculture in hunger prone regions and improving conditions for farm workers and peasants.

Third World governments must also adopt 'food security' policies, designed to ensure first and foremost that there is enough food for their people and that — either through employment schemes, land reform or food subsidies — the poor have access to that food. Agricultural planning should be a careful balance between this paramount objective and the other important, but secondary, objective of producing export crops to earn foreign exchange for other purposes. The Western world — in particular the EEC — should assist Third World governments by respecting their 'food security' policies and not undermining them; by giving aid to agriculture — especially geared to food production in vulnerable areas, and by ensuring that the export crops command a fair and stable price.

Above all, in reforming its agricultural policy the EEC must pay special attention to the impact of those changes on the Third World and in particular on the poorest and must vulnerable people.

Pressures for change

There are pressures for change in the CAP from both inside and outside the EEC.

On the inside, the main pressure is cost. The 1986 CAP budget is £12 billion, or £45 per person in Europe. And because the system maintains artificially high prices, the public pays a further cost — paying more for their food than if the CAP did not exist.

Small farmers have complained that most of the benefits have gone to the better-off farmers. The conservation movement complains that the CAP encourages intensive farming with widespread use of harmful chemicals, mechanisation, cutting down of hedgerows and other uncountable costs to the environment. And the USA and other countries complain that the subsidised EEC exports break international trade agreements and risk starting a trade war. Unless the CAP is changed, the US is set to join battle, with a $2 billion plan to subsidise US farm exports.

Moreover there is public indignation at the way that the main beneficiaries of the CAP appear sometimes to be the Soviet bloc countries. In 1985 the USSR benefited from more than seven million tonnes of cereal sold at highly subsidised rates, as well as cut price butter.[13] The EEC taxpayer undoubtedly spent more in 1985 helping out the Soviet Union with EEC surpluses than famine stricken Africa.

It could be that food surpluses are a problem of the eighties and that agricultural policies will be reformed to do away with them. It is possible that industrialised countries will see a new generation of crops, for instance producing protein-rich animal feed, and new non-food uses for existing surpluses, such as converting them to vehicle fuel. These innovations will reduce the mountains. But as things stand today, massive surpluses are features on the landscape that are costly not only to people in the developed world, but also to people in the Third World.

The way forward

It is easier to say what is wrong than to say what should be done. The CAP is an immensely complicated instrument and there are pressures to reform from many directions. Oxfam is concerned that in the discussions leading up to these reforms the effect on the Third World is actively considered. For this reason Oxfam has initiated a major study with members of the National Farmers Union to weigh up to the pros and cons to the Third World of all the major reform proposals.

The goal

To reform the EEC's Common Agricultural Policy so that it is no longer wasteful and draining on the world's natural resources and so that it no longer creates uncertainty in the world food market. A reformed European agricultural policy should contribute to a goal of food security for all and stability in the prices of the major commodities produced or needed by the world's poor.

How the British Government and the EEC could help

1. Reform the CAP so that its principal objective is to ensure a stable supply, in relation to demand, of the major commodities. This would contribute to price stability in the world market for agricultural commodities. The present practice of the CAP seriously destabilises prices to the disadvantage of Third World producers (and probably smaller farmers in Europe).

2. Concentrate on using land to grow for Europe's needs rather than produce surpluses that are destroyed or wastefully used to feed animals. This might include support for the production of high protein crops and timber which Europe currently imports from developing countries and elsewhere. EEC compensation should be given over a transitionary period to Third World countries which lose markets as a result of diversification in Europe.

3. Set up an evaluation unit to look into the effects on the Third World poor of any proposed changes in the CAP and to suggest ways of alleviating the damage. EEC countries' Aid and Agriculture Ministries should support this initiative.

4. Establish the principle of compensation. The CAP is neither designed to help developing countries, nor to harm them. Where there is inadvertent harm done, the EEC should offer compensation. For example if changes in the CAP were to lead to a significant increase in oilseed rape production, compensation should be given to those developing countries which lose their market for vegetable oil as a result.

5. To curb sugar beet production and thereby to phase out the dumping of highly subsidised EEC sugar on the world market. This depresses the world price of sugar to such an extent that many Third World producers who depend on the sugar trade are reduced to exporting at a loss.

DEBT

A Crisis for the Poor

Introduction

"Should we really let our people starve so that we can pay our debts?" asked Julius Nyerere, then President of Tanzania, in March 1985.[1]

The rules of international finance are making the world's poor give a perverse form of 'aid' to the rich. This 'reverse aid' has helped quell the West's problem of inflation, but at the expense of economic collapse and hunger in the Third World.

Debt is the engine which drives scarce but increasing resources from developing to developed countries and its momentum has built up so rapidly that debt payments now eclipse Western aid and loans combined.

Western compassion shown at the peak of the famine in Africa contrasts uncomfortably with today's reality. The countries south of the Sahara are expected for the first time to become net suppliers of resources to the rich world this year.[2] In 1986 the trickle of funds which go to Africa — mostly aid — will be reversed and will turn into a stream of debt payments running the other way.

The flow of resources *from* the developing world as a whole *to* developed countries amounted to $25 billion in 1985.[3] This compares with total *voluntary* aid of $2.8 billion (£2,000 million) from all Western countries.[4] For every pound put in a charity tin, the West's financial institutions take out £9.

The Third World debt crisis has largely been viewed in Britain as a dual problem — for Western bankers and for Latin American governments. But from the Oxfam viewpoint — working with about 3,000 communities of poor people throughout the Third World — the real brunt of the crisis is being borne by the poor themselves. To understand why the poor are suffering, it is necessary to understand first how the debt crisis arose and how it works.

Origins of the crisis

The money-go-round

In 1973 the price of oil quadrupled. While oil-importing developing countries were badly hit by the increase, a completely new problem arose for the oil producers — a money mountain. The oil-producing countries deposited their newly acquired wealth in Western commercial banks, who in turn needed to find new borrowers. For the banks there were big profits to be made. For industrialised countries there was the prospect of economic growth. So a new mood of liberal lending emerged. Bankers positively courted the finance ministers of developing countries. Governments were seen as fairly safe investments, and developing countries always needed more resources.

Debt outstanding and disbursed

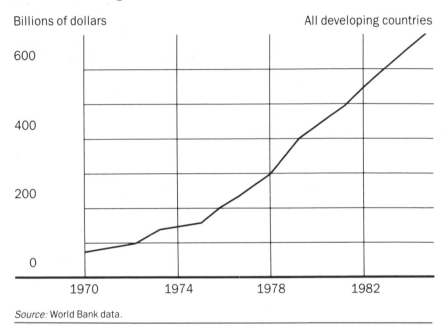

Billions of dollars   All developing countries

Source: World Bank data.

For Third World governments it seemed an answer to their prayers. Bankers were encouraging them to accept more credit.[5] This not only enabled them to borrow to pay for the oil they couldn't afford, but also to embark on ambitious programmes, setting up new industries, building power stations, highways, airports and other prestige developments. It seemed to be a golden opportunity leading to growth and prosperity. Some of the rapidly growing economies of South and East Asia provided a model.

Harsh reality soon dawned, however. As interest rates soared in the late 1970s, the burden of debt payments became heavier and commodities' export prices fell. Growth and prosperity failed to materialise; instead developing countries fell deeper into debt.

From opportunity to crisis

Three international factors conspired to change the economic climate.

1. Oil price rises

In 1973/4 and 1979 oil prices soared, rising from $1.30 per barrel in 1970 to $32.50 in 1981. Increased oil bills accounted for 70% of the increase of Third World debt during the seventies.[6]

2. High interest rates

High interest rates, caused mainly by the US government's budget deficit, forced increased payments onto debtor countries. The US budget deficit currently stands at some $200 billion a year. This creates an immense world demand for capital and, coupled with the tight money supply policies of the leading powers, interest rates have spiralled upwards. Capital, like any other commodity, follows a law of supply and demand, and the price of capital is the interest rate. Although interest rates have fallen in 1986, they are still high in relation to inflation rates in the main economies of the world — especially in Britain.

Long-term interest rates in the United States, 1965–84

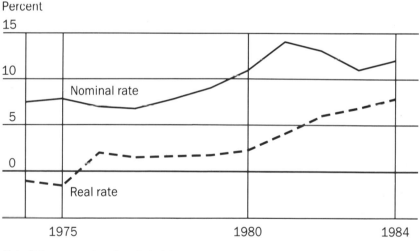

Note: Data are averages of quarterly data.
Source: OECD Financial Statistics and National Accounts: Federal Reserve Board statistical releases.

Ironically, the US government is keen to criticise the bad housekeeping of Third World governments. And the US current account deficit (balance of trade figures with interest charges and services added in) in runs at three times the combined deficit of all developing countries.[7]

3. Recession

World recession has depressed the commodity trade. Prices of the commodities

Case Study — Zambia

The situation in Zambia demonstrates clearly the need for organisations like Oxfam to adjust their work in the light of global economic forces.

Zambia's debt stands at $4.8 billion. Payments on its debts will consume over 70% of its export earnings for the rest of the decade.[15] But its exports are tumbling. The world price of copper, which accounts for 88% of Zambia's exports, fell by 60% in real terms from 1974 to 1984.[16]

As a result Zambia is trying to diversify from copper by rushing into export crop production. Oxfam's representative there, Mike Edwards, describes Zambia as, *"probably the only country in the world trying to move from an industrial to an agricultural base"*.

In order to remain solvent. Zambia has had to borrow heavily through the IMF and in exchange implement a sweeping programme of economic reforms and austerity which, says Mike Edwards, *"is bound to result in greater poverty"*.

The measures included a reduction in government spending, the abolition of subsidies, opening the agricultural market to private enterprise and increasing incentives for export.

With spending cuts, the health service is under great strain. The Ministry of Health has only been allocated one seventh of the budget it needs for importing essential drugs.[17]

A particularly dramatic step was to institute a Foreign Exchange Auction to determine the value of the currency, the Kwacha. The result has been a plummet from K2.2 to the US dollar in October 1985 to K7.3 per dollar by May 1986 — a 70% devaluation.[18]

The currency had been over-valued, but perhaps the devaluation should have been carried out over a period of years, not in a few days. The result has been that fertiliser and fuel prices have doubled, and maize meal has gone up 80% in two months, hitting the urban poor in particular.

depended on by developing countries fell by 25% between 1980 and 1982 and the demand for them has slumped.[8]

The Third World now has to export more than ever to pay for the same amount of imports. The average price of commodities (excluding oil) fell a further 11% in 1985, leading to the lowest recorded price level.[9]

For Western countries the 1985 price cuts saved them $65 billion per year.[10] Twice as much as they give as aid.

Third World responsibility

A large part of the foreign debt has been used to finance a boom in prestige projects and imported goods (as in Chile), to pay for armaments (as in Argentina), or has vanished in 'capital flight' (as in Mexico).[11] Capital flight is

Some of the changes give rural people more money, but the economy is now in such a state that there's nothing to spend it on. Moreover in the remoter areas the farmers are likely to be worse off, because wholesalers are less willing to buy the food grown in these regions and will pay lower prices.

For Oxfam, working in a hostile economic environment with community projects scattered around the country can seem like flying in the face of a hurricane. The importance of this work, however, is that it is not *"doing things for the poor"*, instead it is giving just a bit of help so that poor people can achieve their own ambitions. They don't need ideas imposed from the outside, but they may need help in developing their own ideas and efforts to survive.

In a country like Zambia the resources of voluntary agencies are a drop in the ocean. But, well targeted, they can still have quite an impact. Government services are obliged to adjust rapidly to much reduced budgets. They can learn from the existing efforts of community groups how to stretch their slender resources a long way.

It is hoped, for example, that the health projects Oxfam supports will inject into the official service methods for providing effective but cheap primary health care to poor people. Community mobilisation work may catalyse a new approach to the organisation of local government. And work with groups of poor peasants in the vulnerable areas should encourage local agricultural officers to evolve a more appropriate pattern of agriculture.

The world of Metal Exchanges and the International Monetary Fund is far removed from that of Oxfam, but the impact spreads to the poorest people in the remotest villages. Oxfam's programme in Zambia must evolve to respond to that impact.

particularly pernicious. It has been estimated that between $6–$10 billion of the $26 billion debts of the Philippines, for example, is money exported from the country by the Marcos family.[12] And from 1979 to 1982 it is estimated that some $60 billion was syphoned out of Mexico, Argentina and Venezuela alone.[13]

To blame the Western banks and Northern governments entirely for the debt crisis would be to conceal the very real contribution made by Third World governments and elites.

The Banks

For bankers, debt is a crisis of confidence: confidence in the solvency of the banks. The banks lent huge sums of money to developing countries; more than their own capital. While confidence was high, they could preserve the impression that they were doing well because their competitors were prepared to lend new money to pay the interest on old debts. They did nicely.

But from 1982 onwards that confidence to lend has crumbled. The dramatic turning point in that year was when Mexico called together its creditors and told them that it only had enough reserves in its central bank to pay for 12 minutes worth of imports. By the end of that year, five countries in Latin America (Mexico, Brazil, Venezuela, Argentina and Chile) owed the banks $188 billion and seemed unable to repay.[14]

Governments of the powerful industrialised countries suddenly feared that the entire international banking system might collapse if the major debtor countries declared themselves in default, because the banks no longer had enough reserves of capital to cover Third World loans. In effect the banks would owe depositors more than they had in their vaults. They would be insolvent.

The debt crisis was born.

Reverse aid

Traditionally developing countries have largely depended for their economic growth on resources from the developed world in three forms: official aid, government loans and commercial bank loans. These 'flows' are balanced by debt payments, which comprise capital repayments plus interest charges. In 1983 the balance shifted. The flows out from Third World countries became greater than the flows in; there was a net transfer from poor to rich countries of $11 billion. By 1985 this 'reverse aid' had risen to between $16 and $25 billion per year.[19]

Many economists, and the World Bank, argue that there is little hope of economic growth in developing countries while they are having their resources drained in this way.

The flow could be stopped either by cutting the outgoings (which means changing the rules of international finance) or by increasing the inward flow (which could mean risking yet more loans, leading to an even deeper debt crisis in the future). There's no easy solution, but the flow must be stemmed before the developing countries are bled dry.

Until recently this phenomenon was largely confined to Latin America, which suffered a net drain of $33 billion in 1985, while the rest of the developing world made a net resource gain.[20] But 'reverse aid' is spreading. Sub-Saharan Africa saw an average in-flow of over $10 billion per year from 1980–83. This dropped dramatically to below $2 billion in 1985 and is expected to become a negative flow in 1986.[21] The table opposite compares 1982 and 1985.

Largely because commercial and official loans made in the past are now due for repayment, supplies of credit have dried up, and aid has stagnated — in spite of the world's professed concern for the victims of famine — Africa is on course to be a net supplier of funds to the wealthy half of the world. This is a financial strain that could kill all prospects for economic recovery.

Resource flows to Sub-Saharan Africa[22]
(Figures = billion dollars)

IN	1982	1985
Official Transfers (Grant Aid)	3.1	3.6
Gross borrowing (from governments and banks, and direct investments)	12.4	9.9
Other	3.3	0.3
OUT		
Capital Repayments	−3.2	−7.3
Interest Payments	−3.2	−4.8
BALANCE		
Net Resources Flow	12.6	1.7

The depth of the crisis

Three factors ensure that developing countries cannot cope with their debts.
Exports — commodity prices have tumbled and the demand for commodities has fallen because of world recession.
Imports — in contrast, the price of manufactured goods imported by developing countries has continued to rise steadily.
Finance — with interest rates remaining high, and previous loans needing repayment, the result is a flow of funds from poor countries to rich.

The special case of Africa

International attention has focused on the large debts of countries like Brazil and Mexico. However, the crisis is felt more deeply by the poorest countries, particularly in Africa. Their debts consume a far higher proportion of their national budget. By 1984 sub-Saharan Africa had accumulated total debts of at least $80 billion.[24] Some economists put the figure much higher, at over $100 billion.[25] Africa's debt payments have tripled from $4 billion in 1981 to an estimated $11.7 billion in 1986.[26] As official aid levels stagnate, Africa's fragile economies cannot take this strain. As President Nyerere of Tanzania said, *"if African governments are really representing their people, they cannot accept conditions which would lead to more hunger, to social chaos, to civil war, or to the use of armies against their people"*.[27]

The Banks

Though some banks which lent heavily to developing countries have experienced genuine difficulties in recent years, most of the world's major banks continued to do well as the debt crisis unfolded. For example, Citicorp, a

All developing countries

Total Third World debts stood at $130 billion in 1973 and rose to $1010 billion in 1986. Seven countries — Brazil, Mexico, Argentina, Venezuela, South Korea, Philippines and Indonesia — accounted for 44% of all debts in 1985.

Debt service/exports

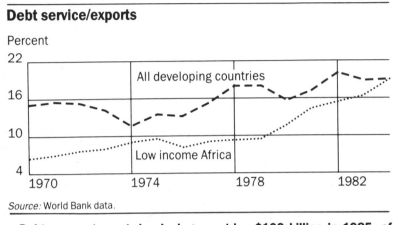

Percent

Source: World Bank data.

Debt payments cost developing countries $102 billion in 1985, of which $52 billion was interest charges. This compares with official aid from all sources of $23.4 billion (in 1984). For non-oil exporting countries the interest bill rose five times from 1977 to 1984, by which time it consumed almost one seventh of all export earnings.[23]

major commercial lender to Brazil, announced 'its best year ever' in 1983 with a record 19% increase in earnings.[28] These loans are many times more profitable than the rest of Citicorp's operations, yielding 20% of the bank's profits, though accounting for less than 5% of its loans.

The risk faced by a bank can be seen in terms of its 'exposure' in the big four Latin American countries; Mexico, Brazil, Argentina and Venezuela. A bank's 'exposure' is its total loans (or 'assets', in banking parlance) to these countries as a percentage of its own capital. Since banks lend considerably more than their own capital, this figure frequently exceeds 100%. The exposure in these Latin American countries of Manufacturers Hanover — a bank which caused a panic in financial circles when it came close to collapse in 1984 — was 173% in that year. The bank had lent one and three quarter times its own capital to these countries.

British banks have lent smaller amounts of money to Latin America, but since they are smaller institutions than the main US banks, the exposure can be equally serious. Lloyds and the Midland are most at risk with exposure in the 'big four' countries of 165% and 205% respectively in 1984.[29]

Handling the crisis — rescheduling

Commercial banks recognised that to avoid a disaster they would have to lend more merely to enable the debtor countries to keep up their interest payments, and to maintain their repayment timetable, often to the very same banks. Their line was that some countries had managed their affairs badly, and they must now 'adjust their economies' by introducing strict austerity measures.

This 'rescheduling' of loans is a credible mechanism for helping the occasional debtor in temporary difficulties, but as pointed out by a Commonwealth Group of Experts led by Lord Lever, *"Rescheduling is simply a way of postponing the day of default at the cost of a bigger default when it comes".*[30]

The rescheduling of loans is often negotiated by the International Monetary Fund (IMF). The condition of rescheduling demanded of debtor countries is to draw up with the IMF programmes of adjustment to their economies. These adjustments include measures which control imports by increasing their price through devaluing the currency. The IMF expects as a result that local consumers will be encouraged to buy local substitutes for imports which have suddenly become more expensive, and in addition that producers will be encouraged to produce more crops for export. In simple terms, the IMF adjustment programmes have the effect of encouraging poor countries to increase export earnings by expanding export crop production; to cut back on imports to save foreign exchange; and to reduce public spending. All such programmes aim to improve the balance of trade — generating surpluses so that banks can be paid their interest.

Even a cursory look reveals a flaw in the logic of this prescription. It is simply not possible for all debtor countries to increase their exports and cut their imports. The result has been a chronic over-supply of raw commodities — such as sugar, tin and palm oil — in relation to demand and consequently a tumbling of the world prices of those commodities. In addition, the IMF's prescriptions are disastrous, because in many debtor countries there are no local substitutes for imports. Overall, the real aim of the IMF is to ensure that the economies of debtor countries integrate with the world economy — itself highly unfair, as the rich countries themselves do not follow the free market practices which the IMF attempts to impose on the debtor countries.

The effect on the poor

The highest price of the debt crisis is being paid by the world's poor; by those who can least afford to pay. Their wages (if they have been able to keep jobs) have fallen steeply in relation to the cost of living. The cost of their basic food has soared as, for instance, government subsidies have been lifted. Expenditure on health care, education and other social service systems has been cut right back. The international problem of recession has become, in its cruellest manifestation, a crisis of hunger for millions of people.

As Cardinal Arns, Archbishop of Sao Paulo in Brazil, said, *"every time the United States raises its interest rates, thousands die in the Third World, because money that would be used for health care and food is sent outside these countries to pay the debt".*[31]

The international economic system has functioned as a conduit channelling recession from the developed to the developing countries, then within the developing countries from the wealthier to the poorer groups.

And within the poorer groups, the main burden has been passed yet again from the men to the women. Economic pressures have increased the male migrant labour force, leaving millions of women to look after the children and earn the household income. Moreover intensive farming for cash tends to squeeze women — who do most of the farm work — from the decision making processes.

In the 1960s those concerned with development coined an optimistic theory of 'trickle-down'. Even if aid and development achievement wasn't targeted accurately at the poor it was argued, it could help to generate economic growth. This wealth wouldn't stay with the better off, but would 'trickle down' so that even the poorest would benefit. Practice has shown however, that wealth created among the elite of a developing country is more likely to be spent in the U.S.A. or Japan than in the local market place, on goods made by the poor.

Jamaica[32]

Although a small country, Jamaica's debt, standing at around $3.2 billion, is enormous, and is considerably more per person than the debt of Brazil or Mexico. An Oxfam report published in 1985 describes how 40% of Jamaica's export earnings are spent servicing the debt, and how — as a result of five IMF negotiations since 1977 — the government has introduced a series of austerity measures with disastrous effects on poor people.

Economic deterioration and escalating unemployment (up to 30% in 1984) have been fuelled by the collapse of the market for Jamaica's principal export, bauxite.

Price controls and subsidies have been removed, wage restraint has been introduced and there have been savage cuts in public spending, particularly hitting the health and education services.

Basic food prices rose 61% in 1984, while a third of the labour force now earns less than £5 per week. There has been a sharp increase in both rural and urban malnutrition, and 28% of under four year olds are now malnourished.

The cuts have led the government to turn some of the agriculture, marketing and even health services over to the private sector. Several health care projects have been referred to Oxfam. One group applying for support wrote the following: *". . . unfortunately, the primary health care service has been cut significantly, due to the current economic situation. The reduction in Community Health Aides has resulted in the deterioration of health care, particularly for the poorer section of society. In one poor suburb of 20,000 people only one Health Aide remains . . . Anaemia in pregnant women has increased from 23% in 1981 to 42% in 1983".*

They continued, *"normally we raise money locally from commerce and industry, but this is now very difficult, due to the decline in sugar, tourism and the economy".*[33]

Chile[34]

Until 1973 Chile was known as 'the Switzerland of Latin America', with a standard of living similar to Britain's. *"Now it's working slowing towards the typical picture of a Third World country",* points out Audrey Bronstein, Oxfam's Country Representative.

The military government has not only curtailed people's human rights, but has also imposed a harsh regime of economic austerity, while accumulating a $20 billion debt, one of the largest in the world. With the onset of the debt crisis in 1982, and following the collapse in copper prices, the Chilean government had to negotiate with the IMF to have its debts rescheduled. As a result, a package of economic 'reforms' was introduced. The impact of these on the poor is familiar. The purchasing power of the minimum wage dropped by a third between 1982 and 1985. One in three people now live below the officially recognised minimum subsistence level. Unemployment has risen steeply, with many men quitting home in search of work, leaving the women to cope by themselves. In the bitter winters the poor can no longer afford fuel, diseases like TB are on the increase and queues outside clinics grow as the health service is cut. The housing problem is also on the increase, with 80,000 homeless people in Santiago and one and a half million more now living in sprawling shanty towns.

Two studies by project workers in the slum areas of Santiago show, respectively, that 62% and 85% of those surveyed could not afford the minimum required diet. Audrey Bronstein describes the increasing occurrence of children fainting from hunger at school. *"But it's an industrialised country and people aren't used to this hardship",* she said, *"It's like acute poverty and hunger coming to Britain".*

The resistance and anger of the poor is increasing rapidly, in spite of the harsh repression of the military police. They were joined in protest by the miners' Trade Unions and by many factory workers in a massive national strike in July 1986.

Tanzania

Tanzania is in particular difficulties. In 1983 its exports were $480 million. Out of this it had to try to pay an oil import bill of $350 million, a debt service bill of over $200 million and about $700 million of other imports. Even after receiving $620 million in aid, Tanzania slipped even further into debt. For the rest of the 1980s Tanzania is scheduled to pay out 60% of its export earnings just servicing its debts.[35] Of course it simply cannot do this; it will have to borrow more —.extending its debt crisis further into the future.

An Oxfam report published in 1985 describes how the agricultural authorities in Tanzania are trying to persuade their farmers to grow cotton for export in totally unsuitable areas (particularly the drought prone Central Region) in order to help pay this debt.[36] Fertilisers are only made available for the cotton crop and the state marketing organisations offer the farmers a far higher price for cotton than for food. There has been a rapid increase in areas planted with cotton, but the average yields per acre have gone down steeply, because the land — which once grew drought-resistant staple foods — is simply not suitable for cotton.

The fight-back begins

Until 1985 the commercial bankers and the IMF were largely satisfied with their case-by-case approach. The big Latin American debtors seemed to be toeing the line.

But in many countries social unrest grew in response to unemployment, spiralling prices and cuts in health and welfare spending and food subsidies. There have been 'IMF' riots in Peru, Jamaica, Sudan, Turkey and elsewhere following the fall in income of urban workers; and there have been many cases of poor mothers, in the slums of Brazilian cities, raiding supermarkets to feed their families. The poor are demonstrating their resistance to continuing and deepening austerity measures.

The governments of the debtor countries, especially where democratic governments have recently taken over from dictatorships, are increasingly fighting against enforced austerity.

Brazil

President Sarney has said:[37] *"We cannot pay the debt with democracy. . . We cannot pay the debt with a hunger of our people. . . Brazil is not an economic risk, but a political risk"* — as a result of austerity measures which have had a harsh effect on the poor.

Sarney proceeded to anger the IMF by ignoring its warning and instituting a $2.5 billion of programme of poverty relief.[38]

Peru

President Alan Garcia, mindful of growing social tension, has rejected IMF demands and told Peru's creditors that the country will pay its $14 billion debts in its own time, restricting debt service payments to 10% of its export earnings each year.[39]

Nigeria

President Babangido has similarly broken off negotiations with the IMF and limited debt payments to 30% of export earnings each year.[40]

Philippines

Mrs. Corazon Aquino announced, even before her election to office, that the Philippines economy, *"cannot possibly endure, nor our people long accept, a situation where nearly half our export earnings must go to interest payments alone".*[41]

Mexico

Mexico, facing lost earnings with the falling price of oil on the world market, has also rebelled over its interest repayments, which currently consume about half of its export earnings.[42]

The 'can't pay, won't pay' attitude is strengthening amongst the bigger debtors. Five Latin American countries (Brazil, Mexico, Argentina, Venezuela and Colombia) have pledged to form a bloc to lobby for a new international approach to the handling of their debt crisis.[43] Fidel Castro of Cuba goes further and advocates an orchestrated joint default.

A view from the North

With the level of debts soaring, increasing numbers of defaults or threatened defaults, and deepening social unrest in the face of enforced poverty, banks and Western governments are beginning to recognise the need for a new approach. The commercial banks are harbouring increasing resentment that governments of the industrialised countries are leaving them to shoulder too much responsibility for the debt crisis. Two hundred of them have called on the IMF and World Bank to supply more money to debtor countries.[44]

The World Bank itself has become increasingly outspoken on the need to find a new approach to debt. *"The economic future of the developing countries, saddled as they are with such large debts, is disquietingly dependent on policy makers in the industrial nations"*, states the World Bank Development Report of 1985.

Many economists, including those in the World Bank, believe that the debt crisis is hampering economic growth in the developed countries, and industrialists are worried about declining exports to developing countries. A recent UNCTAD report has shown that the trimming of imports by the major debtors from 1982 to 1984 has caused the loss of two to three million jobs in Europe and North America.[45] The majority of these losses have been in Europe.

Cheaper oil

In 1985 and 1986, because of a fall in oil prices, the debt crisis has eased a little. The cost of one of the major imports of most poor countries has decreased and interest rates have fallen a few percentage points.

If interest rates fell considerably, and provided oil prices were to remain low, the debt burden of most developing countries would clearly be reduced (although the picture is black for countries such as Mexico and Nigeria which depend on oil exports).

However, the present conditions are unlikely to last forever, and current interest rates in the rich world are still high in relation to inflation. With continuing low prices for their exports debtor countries will still have difficulty meeting the interest payments on debts, and most developing countries will remain in the debt trap.

A new way for debt

Because of the debt crisis, the poor are getting steadily poorer. And this will continue unless a radically new approach is adopted to the handling of the crisis.

The cost of doing nothing, of maintaining an economic regime that makes the poor pay as dearly as they do at present, is intolerable.

An enormous number of solutions have been proposed to the debt crisis. Some of the more important schools of thought are described in Appendix III.

Below is the outline of a new approach, borrowed heavily from these schools of thought. The prescription is a radical one, and demands the active support of governments in both North and South. The starting point must be the acceptance by those governments of a new set of political priorities with the goal of protecting the poor from today's debt crisis.

The goal

To remove the burden of the debt crisis and crippling interest rates from the shoulders of the poor; to turn away from 'austerity measures' which compound hunger and poverty; to allow developing countries the 'economic space' to grow and develop and to allow those countries to be more in control of their own economic destinies.

How Western Governments could help

1. Increase the flow of finance to the developing countries by:—

a) International agreement to reduce to zero the present net transfer of finance from developing countries to the 'North'. This target would demand additional resources amounting to $20–30 billion per year;[46] a huge sum, but less than half a percent of the GNP of OECD countries. Part of this would come from increased aid flows, and part from new commercial bank loans, but under tightly controlled circumstances.

b) Ensuring tighter supervision of future commercial bank lending, and requiring the banks to bear a greater share of the burden for past debts. A mechanism for this would be for governments and the World Bank to offer guarantees for new loans. In exchange the banks would be charged to write off a portion of their bad or doubtful debts each year over a long period.

c) Establishing special mechanisms to respond to the financial needs of the poorest countries, particularly in Africa, without *political* strings attached. Some schemes have already been started, such as the World Bank's Special Facility for Africa and the reactivating of the IMF's Trust Fund. These impose heavy conditionality on the recipient country.

d) Responding to the request from developing countries for a special issue of IMF funding (special Drawing Rights). This is particularly sought by developing countries, as it is finance that does not have to be repaid.

2. Reduce the burden of debt and high interest rates by:—

a) Agreeing an interest rate target for all developing countries no more than 1 or 2% above the world inflation rate. This could be achieved in part by changing Western economic policies (such as the U.S. government exercising greater control over its budget deficit) and in part by an agreement between governments and banks to subsidise the interest rates for developing countries. This degree of subsidy could be linked to the level of poverty and deterioration of terms of trade in the developing country. And rather than be given unconditionally it could be linked to development and welfare programmes agreed with the debtor countries.

b) Early fulfilment of the international agreement to write off the government to government debts of the 36 least developed countries. Britain has a good record in this respect, but other major countries, notably the USA and USSR, have taken very little action. Debtor countries which are slightly wealthier should be allowed to repay part of their debts in their own currencies rather than in foreign exchange.

c) Allowing longer periods for the repayment of loans; multi-year rescheduling replacing the current practice of expecting 'adjustment' to be achieved in a matter of months.

d) Until the debt burden is reduced, responding sympathetically to those developing countries who unilaterally set a ceiling on their debt service charge. This ceiling might be 20% of export earnings for most countries or 10% for countries in particularly extreme financial difficulty. Western governments and commercial banks could help share the debt service burden in these cases.

3. Ease the IMF's handling of the debt crisis along the lines suggested by UNICEF to ensure that any 'economic adjustment' that may be necessary within a developing country:—

a) Does not force cuts of basic services, such as health and education, that benefit the poor. Special credits should be made available, linked to the extension of basic services.

b) Encourages food self-sufficiency and protects the food security of the poor by preserving the production of locally needed food, by ensuring that the urban poor have access to reasonably priced food (subsidised if necessary) and at the same time ensuring that farmers receive good prices and have access to an efficient market.

c) Includes a careful monitoring of the health and nutrition levels of the poor, with contingency plans built in to counteract any slippage in these levels.

d) Includes measures to protect the environment (for example special credits for reafforestation schemes) and preserves accessory spending on environmental protection.

e) Erects firm barriers to 'capital flight' and instead encourages a return of capital previously exported by the wealthy to tax havens and elsewhere.

f) Explores all possible avenues for balancing books by raising taxes on the wealthy, before cutting services relevant to the poor.

g) Concentrates on trimming expenditures that are less relevant to the poor, such as defence, urban highways, and subsidies on state airlines.

4. Allowing developing countries greater control over their own economic destinies by:—

a) Increasing their voting power in the IMF and World Bank.

b) Handling the debt crisis by generating economic growth, rather than austerity and deflation, and fostering that growth in all sectors, not just through the export of raw commodities.

Tasks for Britain

1. UK aid is often given on the condition that an IMF 'adjustment' package is agreed to and implemented. Such conditionality should be changed radically in the same way as is proposed for IMF conditionality.

2. The UK is a major shareholder in the World Bank and IMF and also one of the 'Big Five' Western countries. The government should use this powerful influence to call for major and urgent tallks on the reform of the IMF, reducing interest rates, easing the rescheduling of loans, mobilising new financial resources for developing countries and setting up new institutions and economic policies to solve the debt crisis.

3. The government should complete the writing off of its outstanding loans to the least developed countries. This comprises just over £6 million to South Yemen, Kampuchea, Laos and Vietnam. Since the British government has a good track record in this respect, it should also urge other governments — notably the USA and USSR — to follow suit.

4. The government should, through its Export Credit Guarantee Department, offer to guarantee new loans from UK banks to developing countries in exchange for a commitment from them to write off part of their existing loans.

ARMS

Whose Defence?

"Where mass hunger reigns, we cannot speak of peace. If we want to get rid of war, we must ban mass misery too. Morally, it makes no difference whether human beings are killed in war or condemned to death by starvation. The international community — in the dual sense of concerned citizens and responsible governments — has no more important task, besides controlling the build-up of arms, than overcoming mass hunger and other sources of misery which could be avoided."
Willy Brandt, 1986.[1]

Introduction

Under the guidance of the World Health Organisation, teams of scientists and paramedical workers from around the world worked together in an unprecedented 20 year war. Their enemy was the killer disease smallpox. Eventually they won by rigorous scanning and case follow-up. They eradicated the disease. The cost of this remarkable battle is, coincidentally, the same as the world spends on its military every hour of every day of every year.[2]

And for the price of a single Hawk fighter plane — of which British Aerospace have sold about 100 in recent years to developing countries — it would be possible to provide one and half million people with clean, safe water supplies.

But how practical are comparisons such as these? Is there the remotest chance that if there could be international agreement to shave off a tenth of one percent from world defence budgets — for this is all it would take — we could hope to see in its place a massive immunisation programme to protect every child in the world from the six main killer diseases? It may be argued that there is no economic logic to bring it about; nonetheless there is clearly an overwhelming moral imperative.

The Brandt report, TV documentaries and popular campaigns have focused attention on the contrasting world spending on defence and development. They argue that the two are connected, that high military spending actually reduces development spending. This is one of the hidden costs of the arms race, paid by the poor.

The cost of war

Since peace was declared in 1945 there have been some 120 wars.[3] Almost all of them have been fought in the Third World. In total, eighteen and a half million lives have been lost.[4] Millions have had to flee from their homes, either to live elsewhere in the country or to join the swelling ranks of refugees. In the war-scarred continent of Africa in 1985 there were some four million refugees (one million in Sudan alone) and some six million more displaced from their homes.[5]

Civil war has affected a third of the countries of Sub-Saharan Africa during the last ten years. The continent has seen 20 major armed conflicts since colonial days, the majority of which stem from the rather arbitrary way in which national boundaries were drawn in that period and from the destabilising influence exerted by South Africa.

There is a close correlation between the occurrence of drought and famine on the one hand, and war and conflict on the other, as the map demonstrates.

Africa under stress: the overlap of war, drought and apartheid 1984

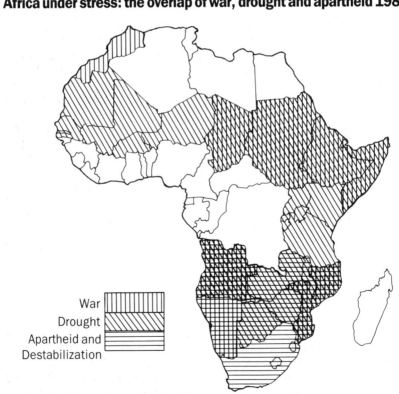

War
Drought
Apartheid and
Destabilization

Source: UNICEF Eastern and Southern Africa Regional Office, Nairobi.

Ethiopia, Sudan, Mozambique, Somalia and Chad are the countries which have witnessed some of the fiercest fighting in Africa in recent years. It is no coincidence that these countries have also seen the severest effects of drought. The drought from 1982–84 was severe by any standards, but had these countries not been fighting major wars they would potentially have had a far greater capacity to cope with the drought and to avoid major famine.

In addition, in all these countries, to a varying degree, the war effort has hampered relief. Food convoys have not been able to get through to the starving. Ships loaded with emergency aid have been held waiting while cargoes of military supplies were unloaded. Civilian diesel supplies ran out to keep the tanks rolling. And emergency health centres have been bombed and shot at.

The lost opportunity cost

Most governments would prefer to see their people free from disease and hunger, but some do little to achieve this. The allocation of spending between defence and social services is a question of priorities. Some governments, perhaps urged on by the IMF, see the need to cut public expenditure as the top priority. They may want to tackle their domestic problem of poverty, but they have decided to get their book-keeping right first. Other governments are preoccupied with wars, civil strife, or the destabilising influence of powerful and aggressive neighbours. For them, tackling disease must come after fighting the more immediate enemy. In countries where hunger is endemic, governments are often so up to their necks in debt that they cannot find the resources necessary to tackle the causes of hunger. But hunger isn't just a problem for the governments of developing countries. As Live Aid has proclaimed, it is a problem we must all share — governments and public, rich nations and poor. With this in view, repeated proposals have been made within the United Nations — as far back as 1955 — to transfer a proportion of each country's military spending into a development fund.

There is no guarantee that funds freed from military expenditure would immediately be applied to the relief of poverty; but to maintain present levels of arms spending is to lose a vital opportunity to realise the moral imperative of eradicating hunger.

In the rich world

To tackle the causes of hunger costs money. At a time when governments of the richer countries are trying to foster growth and cut inflation, they will not want to find the resources for a massive aid programme to combat hunger by increasing public sector borrowing. And cutting health, education and other elements of social spending might prove politically unacceptable and financially unsound. Defence spending is at least a candidate for cuts. It represents, in most countries, a massive pool of resources. A cut in the budget

Case Study — Nicaragua[6]

The 'Contra' guerilla war in Nicaragua is not only killing thousands of people and destroying tens of thousands of homes, but it is also wrecking the development efforts of the Nicaraguan people.

Seven thousand civilians were killed by the war in 1983 and 1984, and by 1984 143,000 people had been forced to leave their homes.

The fighting has forced scores of health centres and hundreds of adult literacy centres to close. Over 300 of the country's teachers were killed or kidnapped in 1984.

The war is also draining an already fragile economy. Forty percent of the government's budget and more than half the country's foreign exchange is consumed by it. In 1984 the destruction and production losses amounted to $255 million. The fighting is always most intense at coffee harvesting time — coffee accounting for a third of the country's foreign exchange earnings.

"The Contra war is wreaking havoc with development schemes all over Nicaragua", states Oxfam's Dianna Melrose in her report *'Nicaragua: the Threat of a Good Example?'*. *"It is a senseless diversion from the real war against poverty and under-development"*.

The problems of destruction and financial drain are compounded by the weak economic situation of Nicaragua. The country has a three and a half billion dollar debt — largely a legacy of twenty years' dictatorship under the Somoza family.

World prices for Nicaragua's four principal exports — coffee, cotton, sugar and meat — have all fallen compared to the levels of the late 1970s. In 1970 a 100lb bag of coffee would have bought 100 barrels of oil; by 1982 it was only worth three barrels. Moreover the shortage of foreign exchange is crippling industry and transport.

Oxfam's work in Nicaragua — in the light of the war — has had to change dramatically from development to emergency relief, concentrating on first aid, emergency feeding and resettlement of displaced people.

In 1983 the governments of Colombia, Mexico, Panama and Venezuela — the Contadora group — proposed a peace initiative. They reached agreement with all the Central American governments on five principles for easing the present conflict. These are: halting the arms race, reducing stocks of weapons, ending foreign military involvement, controlling the arms trade and preventing national territory being used to destabilise governments in neighbouring countries.

At present the Contadora peace initiative offers the only hopeful prospect for resolving the conflict in Central America. But if it is to work it needs the backing of Western governments — particularly the USA.

would have relatively little impact on the economy of the country. Studies have shown that defence spending reduces economic growth by draining resources and skills which could be used more productively in other sectors, industry or housing for example.[7] A very high proportion of the world's research scientists are involved in military related projects.

There is also an element of arbitrariness in the size of the defence budget. Other elements of public expenditure — such as Social Security — are budgeted according to measurable needs. It is simply not possible to quantify objectively the *needs* of defence. Hence within Western nations defence budgets range from 1.3% of GNP in Austria, 1.4% in Spain and 1.8% in Italy, to 6% in the USA.[8] And within a given country the defence bill varies markedly from one government to the next.

. . . and in the poor world

The human race has within its power the ability to eliminate hunger, to eradicate the main killer diseases and to provide all basic needs to its members. This precious opportunity is being frittered away. It is not just the bombs that are dropped that cause destruction. The bombs that are bought, stored, displayed proudly in military displays but never dropped, cause destruction just as surely. Is there any evidence for this claim? There are plenty of correlations between indicators of poverty and high military expenditure. For example a comparison of the percentage of a government's budget spent on its military with the percentage on social expenditure (i.e. Education, Health, Housing, Social Security and Welfare combined) and infant mortality rates for three pairs of countries in different regions of the world, shows the following (1982 figures).[9]

Country	% Spent on Military	% Spent on Social	Infant Mortality Rate
Sri Lanka	1.4	23.5	31
Pakistan	33.5	10.1	119
Costa Rica	2.9	69.5	20
El Salvador	11.9	29.0	70
Kenya	13.2	28.0	81
Uganda	19.8	26.6	108

There are, of course many other factors that come into play. A study has been made by health statisticians of the relationship between military spending and infant mortality rates in 141 countries. The conclusion of this research, taking into account other factors, such as overall national wealth, is that there is indeed a strong correlation. The report concludes that two million infant deaths per year may be attributable to military spending, before a single weapon is fired.

Other studies have shown that developing countries with lower military budgets have more thriving economies. Arms spending is an economic drain. An analysis of data from 50 countries showed that high military spending reduced savings and investment, drained human and financial resources, reduced growth and increased debt and inflation.

It would be simplistic to say that all military spending is bad or unnecessary. It is not enough merely to remove the weapons of war; it is essential to address and resolve the causes of war.

The cash cost

Pressure of the Arms Race

Defence policies demand increasingly sophisticated technology; in other words more and more expensive weapons. And it is estimated that military technology has the fastest built in rate of obsolescence.[10] There has been a large increase in the cost of the research and development of such weaponry, and one advanced weapon can now do the job of ten of the previous generation. The domestic arms needs of a major arms producing nation alone are too small to justify the cost, and so there is increasing pressure to sell weapons abroad to bring down the cost to the nation of its own military hardware.

The Mirage III fighter jet illustrates this point. The manufacturer, Dassault, built them essentially for the French airforce, which wanted 200 of them. But by selling 350 of them to overseas customers, the cost to the French government was reduced by 25%.[11]

Superpower rivalry has intensified the quest for increasingly sophisticated weapons and so has accelerated the drive to sell more weapons abroad. The arms race fuels the arms race.

Moreover superpower rivalry has exacerbated many of the conflicts. It is estimated that in well over half the armed conflicts between 1945 and 1975 there was outside intervention from Western powers or the Eastern bloc.[12] This same influence is seen not only in direct intervention, but also in the supply of weapons to the developing world.

Opportunity for Britain

The fact of the matter is that the arms trade is big business for Britain. Arms exports bring in over £2400 million per year (1984).[13] This is not only a major source of foreign exchange, but also helps reduce the defence bill by charging overseas customers a good slice of the research and development costs involved in designing new weapon systems. The UK is the fourth largest arms trader in the world (after the USA, the USSR and France) and some three quarters of our exports go to the Third World.[14]

For example British Aerospace recently secured a repeat order to supply Indonesia with Rapier missiles, a contract worth £82.7 million.[15] Indonesia is the largest debtor country in Asia (1983), the population has a life expectancy of just 54 years and more than one in nine of its children die before the age of five. Indonesia was also the sixth largest recipient of UK aid in 1984, but even this massive aid programme (£28 million) is only a third of the size of the Rapier contract.

The recent sale of HMS Hermes to India at a reported cost of £60 million has been rather more publicised.

Deals like these, the maintenance of the Defence Export Services Organisation — a special government department to help win arms contracts (no other export sector receives anything like this support from the government) — and the lavish spending on arms fairs chiefly aimed at the Third World market all contrast grimly with the real needs of the Third World poor — defence from poverty, injustice and hunger. In 1984, as the African famine unfolded, there were five government sponsored British arms sales missions to sub-Saharan Africa.[16]

Cost for the Third World

Arms spending has to be distinguished from military spending. The former is just the equipment, mainly imported in the case of developing countries, while the latter is everything, including paying the troops.

Arms spending probably only accounts for 10–15% of Third World military budgets, but this has grown steeply since the 1960s. Third World military imports trebled in real terms between 1962 and 1981.[17] The 1980s have seen a decline in the levels of Third World arms imports, because of the general economic crisis, and the replacement of some military dictatorships by less militaristic governments, as well as the evolution of a domestic arms industry in the Third World.

The Third World arms trade stood at about $12 billion in 1982, plus about $2 billion in gifts, mostly from the Soviet Union (which is notably ungenerous in terms of development aid). The $12 billion that has to be paid for is a heavy drain on foreign exchange. It has been estimated that the arms bill accounts for between 15% and 25% of total accumulated Third World debt.[18]

The better-off oil producing developing countries account for most of the arms trade. But although smaller sums are involved, the arms imports of poorer countries can be more damaging to their economies. One third of the value of all imports of machinery and equipment to Africa is arms and military equipment.

Global military spending continues to soar, rising 40% from 1975 to 1985. It now stands at about $800 billion per year, 84% of which is accounted for by the two superpowers.[19] Although the Third World share is relatively small as a proportion of their total government spending, the defence budget is seriously draining in many cases. Africa's military spending rose from $8.5 billion in 1970 to $14 billion in 1982.[20]

Getting on the Band Wagon

The arms trade isn't all one way. As economic problems grip developing countries — particularly major debtors — manufacturing and trading arms is proving doubly lucrative. Not only does it help the economy by displacing imports, but it also gives some of them a chance to earn foreign exchange by becoming arms traders themselves.

Thirty-four developing countries now have their own arms industries and are themselves becoming major arms exporters.[21] Brazil, Egypt and India lead the field. According to 'South' magazine, Brazil's arms sales now amount to $3 billion per year — not far behind the British arms industry. In 1985 the RAF made history by placing an order with Brazil to buy 130 T-27 Tucano military planes — Brazil's first ever arms contract with a NATO country.[22]

The repression cost

A powerful argument for transferring funds from military to development spending — and a case for saying that richer countries *should* share in that transfer and in the responsibility for fighting world poverty — lies in our own self-interest. Poverty and oppression is the breeding ground for much of the conflict in the world. Some 15 major Third World wars are going on today. Almost any of these could escalate and become the stage for future superpower tension. It is in our own interest to defuse these timebombs. To do this demands fighting the poverty and injustice which gives rise to conflict, at the same time redoubling diplomatic initiatives to negotiate peace.

The 'Khmer Rouge' regime of Pol Pot arose in Kampuchea out of the poverty and destruction caused by the Vietnam war. That regime unleashed yet fiercer destruction and tyranny on the Khmer people until it was forced into exile, leaving the legacy of the 1979 famine. It was exiled but not expunged. The Khmer Rouge continues to fight for a chance to seize power once more.

Oxfam, which has worked in the country since 1979, saw first-hand the horrors of the famine, but now witnesses the continuing poverty of the people because of the virtual absence of help from the Western world. Within the United Nations Pol Pot's Khmer Rouge, in uneasy coalition with smaller groups, is still recognised as the legitimate government, because the government of Heng Samrin in Phnom Penh is supported by military forces from Vietnam. Until this political deadlock is resolved, there will be no official aid, and poverty and hunger will continue.[23]

Similarly the chaos and poverty in Afghanistan, with daily food riots and uncontrolled lawlessness, provided an excuse for the Soviet invasion of that country. And elsewhere — in Central America, Sudan, Indonesia, Sri Lanka and many other countries — conflict between different groups of the population threatens the fabric of those societies.

Militarisation of societies has heavy social costs and retards democratic political development. It is invariably a product of military governments.

Increasingly destructive weapons give greater power to the armed forces, power that can be used to further the political ambitions of the military. In 1960 there were approximately 22 military controlled governments. By 1985 the figure had risen to 58, almost half of which are in Africa.[24]

Increasingly, the Third World demand for arms has focused on so-called repressive technology — electric stun batons, water cannon, crowd monitoring and torture equipment — equipment which is largely designed to control civilians. Britain is one of the major suppliers of such equipment. The call for it is clear. As food riots erupt throughout Africa, Asia and Latin America, as angry crowds demand changes in government and as mothers take to looting supermarkets in order to feed their children, those in power seek to cling on to leadership by using all the force they can muster.

It is often *relative* poverty that breeds violence. When one group of the population is discriminated against, it is human nature to fight back.

It might be possible to crush civil unrest by sheer military might. But the only way to eliminate it is by removing the poverty, injustices and divisions that fuel the conflict. It is not a military solution, but social and political solutions, that are required.

It is in the interests of Western governments to work towards this goal, and so help to make a safer, more stable world for everyone, not least for our children and grandchildren.

The way forward

The Third World poor are the main victims of war, the most likely to feel the sting of the repressive technology, and they pay the heaviest price for the debts caused by arms imports.

It would be naive to believe that the arms trade could be switched off easily or quickly. Its scale relates closely to the pace and intensity of the arms race itself. Action by the world's main powers to reduce their own arms budgets is of great and urgent importance for the poor.

The evidence linking the crisis of poverty with current levels of arms spending is too serious to be ignored. It calls for Western government action on three fronts. Firstly to restrain the Third World arms trade, secondly to help resolve existing conflicts peacefully and thirdly to join in a massive international war against the common enemy — poverty.

The goal

To contribute to a transfer of spending from the arms race to development, and to help develop a climate in which there is less conflict and less dependence on arms spending and military might.

How Western Governments could help

1. Urge the superpowers to resist involvement in Third World battlefields, and instead make strenuous efforts to strengthen the peace-making and peace-keeping roles of the United Nations. Exploring all avenues for encouraging the resolution of conflicts through diplomacy rather than military means: the British government's role in helping resolve the conflict in Zimbabwe might serve as a model.

2. Phase out all state subsidies (such as Defence Exports Services Organisation missions and arms fairs) on arms trade with developing countries.

3. Support international efforts to transfer spending from the arms race to development, such as by the establishment of a Disarmament for Development fund as proposed within the United Nations (contributions to which might be levied as a tax on all arms trade and military expenditure).

4. Support other international efforts designed to restrict and monitor international arms trade, such as obligatory disclosure of all arms trade contracts and the strengthening of arms control agreements.

5. Agree restrictions on Third World arms trade, particularly to exclude the supply of repressive arms and equipment likely to be used against civilians.

CONCLUSION

The 1980s are a time *of* change and a time *for* change.

The living conditions of people in developing countries have changed in recent years — mostly for the worse. The international economic scene is in a state of rapid flux as oil prices fall and rise, interest rates surge, world unemployment rises inexorably and the world's leading economy — the USA — jumps to the number one slot in the chart of leading debtors.

In Western countries the public view of world poverty has changed dramatically. Today a full spectrum of British Society is truly anxious to help fight poverty. The foundation for their concern is the traditional motivation of pity for the starving, but reinforced now by the emotion of anger; anger that world leaders are not using the power that we give them to abolish hunger for ever.

Politicians are responding to this new public mood. Not in decades have there been so many debates in Westminster on Third World issues, nor such cross-party concern about the aid record of Western governments.

The British government has responded by stepping up famine relief aid, and aid for post-famine reconstruction in Ethiopia and elsewhere. On the whole the response — paying Paul — has been made possible by robbing Peter. Virtually no new aid funds have been allocated by the government, in spite of the wave of public compassion. Aid to the Indian sub-continent has taken a nosedive to accommodate the new high levels of UK aid to Africa; in the government's aid programme, famine relief has been at the expense of long term development.

Aware of the sea of change that surrounds them, voluntary organisations like Oxfam are also searching for new ways of working. How can they stay silent, working in few and scattered communities, helping to create islands of survival, when all around them conditions of poverty are getting worse and worse? They may feel powerless to do anything that stops the slide directly, but they are realising that they cannot ignore it.

Voluntary organisations are starting to assume a wider role in two senses. Firstly, they are alive to the need to adjust their programmes to take into account the economic forces that fuel poverty. This may involve close contact not just with other non-governmental organisations, but also with official aid agencies and sometimes government departments, in a new colloborative approach to development. At least they must learn to understand what official institutions are doing and the effect of their actions on the poor.

Secondly, voluntary organisations are realising that, in response to the high levels of public and parliamentary concern in their home countries, they must learn to describe their experiences not in isolation, but in the context of the international economic and political environment in which they work. Voluntary organisations are not normally inhibited — nor modest — in describing their achievements. Now they are learning to 'tell it as it is' and to contrast the success stories (vital as they are for the millions of people helped each year by voluntary aid) with the downward slide towards a greater poverty that is the fate of hundreds of millions of people in the Third World today. Now while saying, *"Don't stop the giving,"* they are also saying, *"Stop the taking."*

This book is an offspring of the new outlook being developed by voluntary organisations.

Few in Oxfam are economists or experts in international trade. Oxfam has one unique qualification, however. It has a network of projects, partners and staff which brings it into close daily contact with poor people in thousands of communities throughout the Third World. Oxfam can see clearly how the problem of recession — our problem of Western recession — is filtering down and being magnified, and being borne by the very poorest people on Earth. People who simply don't have the strength to carry this burden.

For Richer, For Poorer attempts to describe how poverty is exported by the wealthier countries — how five major forces connect Britain with the problem of world hunger. It also looks at the opportunities which exist to lessen the damage, at the chances Western governments have to be part of the solution, not part of the problem.

Some would argue that, through generous emergency aid for famine relief in Africa the West has shown how deeply it cares. But even as one arm of government started to respond to the famine, other fingers were picking the pockets of the poor. The Debt Crisis and the crashing prices of raw commodities have wiped out the value of Western aid many times over.

Adding insult to injury, Western governments seek not only to protest their innocence for world poverty, but to throw all the burden of blame onto developing countries themselves. The accusations are in part justified. Third World governments vary enormously and some do display a cynical disregard for their poor. Some make it trivially easy for their wealthy elite to send vast amounts of precious foreign exchange out of the country to swell private bank accounts in Switzerland. Some have indulged in an orgy of prestige development schemes which are shamefully irrelevant to the needs of their people. Others have ignored for far too long the pressing need to devalue their currency or to slim down their government bureaucracies.

The criticisms are valid, and have been admitted by Third World governments themselves. But they are also a smokescreen. The passion with which the accusations are made comfortably conceals a hard truth. The international economic system is itself a major engine of Third World poverty.

True, many Third World governments have made some appalling mistakes, but even if they remained blameless they would still be experiencing unprecedented economic starvation today. Is it reasonable to expect governments of poor countries to withstand — as they had to in 1985:

- A debt burden which topped the $1 billion mark for the first time.
- The US emerging on the debt scene as the world's biggest debtor — greedily soaking up capital and so pushing interest rates sky-high.
- The emergence of "reverse aid" — a flow of $25,000 million from poor countries to rich as debt payments overtake new lending and aid.
- The loss of $40,000 million a year of foreign exchange. Five years of falling commodity prices caused erosion of export earnings equal to 1½ times total Third World aid.
- A further 11% fall of non-oil commodity prices during 1985. Average prices hit the lowest point in the 27 years' history of measuring this index.
- For Africa — the culmination of one of the worst periods of drought in the continent's history.
- For every £1 the world contributed as famine relief Africa was expected to pay back £2 in debt payments.

It is right to level criticism for past errors, but in the face of such obstacles economic survival in itself is quite a feat. For the Third World to have borne this burden of recession without savage human consequences would have been little short of miraculous.

THE WAY FORWARD — A 20 point programme for international reform

The following is a summary of the recommmendations made at the end of the previous five chapters. Some of the proposals are easier to achieve than others. Taken together they would amount to a major set of reforms which would enable the industrialised countries, and in particular Britain, to become part of the solution to world poverty and hunger.

Aid

1. Reduce the commercial emphasis on aid, and in particular cut the Aid Trade Provision.

2. Allocate a much greater proportion of aid to the direct needs of the poor and give special help to the countries which have a good track record in fighting poverty. Explore ways of involving the poor — and in particular women — in the design and operation of aid projects.

3. Increase the emphasis on agricultural development, land reform, 'food security' and on research into food crops suitable for agriculturally vulnerable areas. Increase the emphasis on basic services (such as health and water supplies) needed by the poor, and on environmental protection.

4. Reform food aid so that it does not damage Third World farmers and so that emergency food aid is delivered more swiftly.

5. Agree a five year timetable for British government aid to reach the UN aid target of 0.7% GNP.

Trade

6. Assist the cooperation between developing countries in improving their own trade opportunities.

7. Reduce the barriers to imports from the Third World especially in the case of the poorest countries.

8. Support international efforts to impose ethical controls on international companies and on commodity speculators.

9. Support international efforts to stabilise the prices of commodities on which developing countries depend. Increase the funding for compensation schemes such as STABEX which help guarantee export earnings for developing countries, and make the procedures of these schemes more flexible.

Northern Agriculture

10. Reform the EEC Common Agricultural Policy so that it contributes to stabilising commodity prices in the world market and to producing food Europe needs rather than unwanted surpluses.

11. Monitor the effect of EEC agricultural policies on developing countries and offer compensation when these policies result in loss to the Third World.

12. Curb the overproduction of sugar beet and thereby phase out the dumping of highly subsidised EEC sugar on the world market.

Debt

13. Increase the flow of finance to developing countries with the target of reducing to zero the present transfers of resources from developing countries to the North. A new regime of close supervision of bank lending is called for which places a greater burden of responsibility for the debt crisis on the banks. Special measures are needed to help provide the finance needed by the poorest countries, especially in Africa.

14. Reduce debt payments by taking steps to cut interest rates, writing off the government to government debts of the poorest countries, allowing longer periods to repay past loans and by being sympathetic to developing countries who decide to set a ceiling on their debt payments.

15. Soften the 'austerity measures' which hurt the poor by cutting basic services, undermining 'food security', or by over-exploiting their natural resources. Economic adjustment should include careful monitoring of the impact on the poor and should concentrate on curbing capital flight, taxing the wealthy, refraining from unnecessary 'prestige' development schemes and cutting government spending which is less relevant to the poor.

16. Allow developing countries greater control over their own economic destinies by helping to foster economic growth — rather than austerity — as a solution to the debt crisis and by giving developing countries greater voting power in the IMF and World Bank.

Arms

17. Urge the superpowers to resist involvement in Third World battlefields and instead explore all avenues for encouraging the resolution of conflicts through diplomacy rather than by military means.

18. Support international efforts to transfer spending from the arms race to development, for example by establishing a Disarmament for Development fund as proposed within the UN.

19. Phase out all state subsidies on the arms trade with developing countries and support international efforts to restrict and monitor this trade.

20. Stop supplying developing countries with 'repressive arms' and equipment likely to be used against civilians.

Appendix I

African debt payments calculations

The 29 poorest countries of Sub-Saharan Africa paid back to the West twice as much as they received in emergency aid in 1985. This statement is derived from two separate calculations (1 and 2 below).

Debt statistics are difficult to unravel because they can be quoted in so many different ways, i.e. for different groups of countries or for different types of debt. Furthermore, the actual figures vary from the estimates as interest rates fluctuate, and as debtors default or defer their payments when they cannot meet their commitments.

Emergency Relief

Official aid contributions to the famine relief effort were almost $3 billion in 1985. Voluntary aid amounted to a further $500 million, giving total emergency aid to Africa of about $3.5 billion ('African Emergency Report' No. 7, UN Office for Emergency Operations in Africa, 1986).

Debt Payments

Calculation 1

According to World Bank figures published in April 1986 ('Financing Adjustment with Growth in Sub-Saharan Africa', page 3) debt service payments for the 29 poorest countries were projected at $6.8 billion per year for 1986–90. On the same basis the World Bank projection for 1985 would, if anything, be slightly greater. The figure of $6.8 billion was central to the discussions about Africa's difficulties at the UN Special Session on Africa in May 1986.

Calculation 2

Total debt service payments for Sub-Saharan Africa as a whole amounted to $12.1 billion in 1985 ('African Debt and Financing', Institute of International Economics). About 48% of this debt service is from 28 of the poorest countries (calculated from World Bank debt tables). Adding approximately $0.2 billion debt service for the final country, Mozambique, gives a debt service of $6.0 billion for the 29 countries. Adding $640 million service on IMF credits gives a total debt service figure of $6.7 billion.

Calculation 3

The very latest provisional figures available from the World Bank at the time of going to press (October 1986) indicate a slightly different ratio for debt payment of about £1 to £1.61 out. The ratio is slightly lower, partly because in practice it appears that African countries have simply stopped paying off some of their debts, so cutting down on the out-flows. Such defaulting, however, merely delays the burden of paying till future years.

The total debt service for the 29 poorest countries (latest projections on end of 1984 debt statistics) is calculated by the World Bank's External Debt Division to be approximately $5.64 billion. This indicates short and long-term debts of all kinds and IMF payments.

Appendix II

The Aid Trade Provision (ATP)

The ODA has commissioned a survey of ATP projects which analyses six projects and is believed to be very critical of ATP.[1] But the report has not been published and is covered by the Official Secrets Act.

The government's justification for ATP is that other countries started this credit race. Britain, however, is one of the pacesetters in this sort of export subsidy, though it is true that the government is initiating international discussions on a 'mutual ceasefire'.

Some ODA officials maintain that ATP is a necessary evil, in that it satisfies the industry lobby, who otherwise might be anti-aid. But the Chairman of the group that represents British exporters' views to the government has insisted to Oxfam that this is not so, that exporters are not — as they are often described — anti-aid and that they would naturally prefer it if export subsidies were completely within the Department of Trade and Industry and not a charge on the aid budget.[2] Exporters do want subsidies to be easier to obtain, but they are not necessarily saying that they should come from the aid budget.

Criticism of the ATP has grown in recent years. A Treasury report (the Byatt report of 1983) condemns it as a bad use of public funds. The unpublished ODA survey of selected ATP projects concludes that, *"you can't use the same fork to eat your dinner and to dig your garden with"*.[3] In other words that it is either aid for exporters, or aid for the developing country, not both. The all-party Foreign Affairs Committee of the House of Commons has criticised ATP, and an increasing number of ODA officials are critical of it.[4]

Despite this mounting criticism, the ATP budget is expanding. It has grown from 3% of bilateral aid in 1980 to over 6% in 1984. The 1984 expenditure (£52 million) exceeded the entire budget of Oxfam at the time and was one and a half times the government's aid for disaster relief, food aid and debt crisis support to the whole of sub-Saharan Africa.

Now China is being added to the list of ATP-eligible countries, procedures are being made even easier (to include aid for subsidising bank loans to pay for British contracts) and the budget is expanding further. ATP is being increased by £10 million in 1987/8 and £20 million in 1988/9.

The government has recently responded to public opinion by announcing an increase in the overall aid budget, but if the ATP is deducted, the forward spending projections show a continuing decline in the real value of UK aid.[5]

Appendix III

Ten schools of thought on the debt crisis

1. The Brandt Commission: *North South, Common Crisis* [1]

These two reports argue that the IMF should be less preoccupied with austerity measures and place more emphasis on growth, employment and income distribution. They also argue that debt repayments should be linked to the borrower's capacity to pay. The second Brandt report, *Common Crisis*, specifically calls for a writing off of official (i.e. government to government) debts to the least developed countries, for a new Multilateral Investment Insurance Agency to be formed to promote and guarantee new commercial loans and for greater voting power for developing countries in the World Bank and IMF.

2. Celso Furtado: *No to Recession and Unemployment* [2]

A book examining the Brazilian economic crisis by Celso Furtado, one of the most influential Brazilian economists and Minister of Planning from 1962–63. This report argues that debtor countries should use the weapon of refusing to pay, that they can use this threat to negotiate better terms, and they will get away with it because no party, especially the banks, wants to declare a country in default (which would mean the banks having to write off their assets in that country). Furtado describes as futile the efforts of debtor countries, goaded by the IMF, to produce more and more for export just to continue interest payments to foreign banks. He urges Brazil to break from the IMF stranglehold and to replace austerity with development for a future free from poverty.

3. UN Position on Least Developed Countries

A number of UN meetings and reports have drawn special attention to the acute problems of the 36 poorest or least developed countries. UNCTAD called, as early as 1978, for all industrialised countries to write off their official debts (resolution 165 of UNCTAD's Trade and Development Board). Many countries, notably Britain, have acted on this resolution, but two of the largest creditors — the USA and the USSR — have not. Meanwhile, the debts of the poorest countries continue to soar, increasing by 68% between 1978 and 1982,[3] and now stand at over $26 billion.[4] UN forums continue to point out that without the cancellation of the official debts, or at the very least allowing repayment in the currencies of the debtor countries rather than demanding scarce dollars, there is little economic prospect for the poorest countries.

4. The World Bank

The economic approach of the World Bank has now begun to draw away from that of the International Monetary Fund. The Bank has criticised the rigidity of the IMF austerity approach and has advocated instead a policy of stimulating economic growth.[5] More recently it has stressed the need for poverty-relieving elements to be included in the economic 'adjustment' of debtor countries. The World Bank has urged the IMF to look for longer term solutions, and at a joint World Bank/IMF meeting in April 1985 called for a new era of longer term rescheduling of loans. In Autumn 1985 the President and Vice-Presidents of the World Bank gave their support for the Baker Plan (see no. 7) and called for attention to growth by more effective investment, including improved aid, and for economic reforms of the industrialised countries to reduce the debt crisis.

In a special report on Africa the World Bank drew particular attention to the immense difficulties facing African countries which had seen their debt bill triple in the first four years of the 1980s.[6] The report called for a special new fund for Africa, particularly to help tackle the African debt crisis. In the event only about a fifth of the funds called for were contributed and much of this, such as the British contribution, wasn't even new money, but came from existing aid budgets.

In March 1986 the Bank issued a report on food security, *'Poverty and Hunger'*.[7] This report opens with the paradox that, *"The world has ample food. The growth of global food production has been faster than the unprecedented population growth of the past 40 years. . . Yet many poor countries and hundreds of millions of poor people do not share in this abundance. They suffer from a lack of food security, caused mainly by a lack of purchasing power"*. The report calls unambiguously for a softening of austerity measures. *"When necessary, adjustment programmes should include economically viable measures to safeguard the food security of the most vulnerable groups, particularly children under five and lactating women"*. These are not new arguments. Voluntary organisations, Unicef and others have been using them for years. The importance of this report is that the World Bank, which has in recent years been preoccupied with economic growth along strict Western lines, has chosen to stress that debt causes hunger and that a civilised world must tackle head-on this dual economic and human crisis.

5. The Commonwealth Group of Experts

In 1984 a Commonwealth Group of Experts, comprising mostly Third World economists, under the chairmanship of Lord Lever, painted a vivid and frightening picture of the debt crisis and put forward a strategy for sharing the burden of debt more equitably between governments of North and South and the commercial banks themselves.[8] The proposals rested on renewed investment in developing countries by commercial banks and Northern governments, long-term rescheduling of existing loans, writing off part of both commercial bank and official debts, a reduction of international interest rates and special measures to help the poorest countries.

6. Unicef

The organisation which has given most consideration to the situation of the poorest *people* within the debt crisis is Unicef. In studies of the impact of recession on children, in successive annual reports and in speeches by both the Director and Deputy Director, Unicef has unfolded both the most harrowing account of the human cost of world recession and a comprehensive strategy for safeguarding the poor from continuing suffering. These are brought together in its report *Within Human Reach*, which concentrates on the problems of Africa.[9] It includes a strong criticism of the IMF and World Bank for imposing, *"Draconian austerity measures in the name of economic adjustment"* and argues for a new international and coordinated action on six fronts to meet basic human needs and rebuild *"the human foundation for sustained development"*. The first five fronts relate to development planning and aid policy, the sixth to the debt crisis. The latter recognises that some economic adjustment is necessary, but calls for, *"adjustment with a human face"*, namely adjustment measures that safeguard a minimum nutritional standard for all, that encourage greater food production and income earning opportunities for the poor (especially women), that strengthen basic human services such as health and education (often without necessarily spending any more money) and that protect the fragile environment of Africa. The report calls for cooperation between governments of North and South and the international agencies in adopting this broader approach to adjustment and for a substantially increased flow of resources to Africa, not just in increased aid, but also in the form of better trade opportunities and cutting the debt bill.

7. The Baker Plan

A significant shift in the US government position was announced to the annual meetings of the IMF and World Bank by Treasury Secretary, James Baker, in September 1985.[10] The Reagan administration had previously maintained that the debt crisis hit countries individually, it wasn't a crisis in the international economic order. Consequently, the IMF was right to take a case by case approach, encouraging governments — country by country — to get back into line with their debt payments. The Baker Plan was a major shift from this position in recognising:—

a) that interest rates had to be brought down (notably by eradicating the US government's own budget deficit by 1991)

b) that new resources must be found for the major debtors (in particular $20 billion of new commercial bank loans and $9 billion of World Bank loans over three years). The new loans would, however, only be given in exchange for major commitments by the recipients to 'reform' their economies along classic IMF lines

c) that the poorest African countries need special help (a $5 billion trust fund was proposed)

d) — perhaps most tellingly — that the World Bank, rather than the IMF, should adopt the lead role in handling the Debt Crisis. (The IMF approach previously favoured is essentially to balance books by cutting spending: the World Bank approach can be characterised by balancing books by increasings earnings, i.e. economic growth). The change of heart probably reflected economic self-interest more than a new-found concern for Third World debtors (in particular as US exports to Latin America had fallen by about 40%). Also of significance is the fact that the US itself has become a major debtor (in fact eclipsing all other countries' debts). Its major banks are beginning to suffer losses as a result of the debt crisis, and so it has recognised the real dangers of a series of major defaults to its own banking system.

The Baker Plan has been received quite warmly by other Western governments and more cautiously by commercial banks. They would prefer to reduce their exposure in the Third World, but they realise this isn't feasible. So their response to Baker has been, *"we'll go along with it, as long as everyone else does"*. Their share of new lending would be about £1 billion but, they have argued, measures must be taken to stop a capital flight (the transferring of funds by wealthy Third World elites, such as the Marcos family of the Philippines, into tax havens or US real estate). So far the Baker Plan has not got very far. By August 1986 there had been just one new loan under the proposed scheme (a $698 million World Bank loan to Mexico) and this was still uncertain. At least one major bank (Morgan Guaranty) has warned that the plan will be stillborn unless speedy action is taken.

8. The Latin American Governments

The Finance Ministers of the major Latin American debtors — the so-called Cartagena Group — meet regularly to coordinate their response to the debt crisis. They have studiously avoided presenting themselves as a debtors' cartel or threatening simultaneous default, but they have become increasingly insistent that the industrialised countries must do more to help. In December 1985 they met to discuss the Baker Plan, and their verdict was, essentially, that it was a step in the right direction, but nowhere near enough.[11] They agreed a counter-proposal which heavily modifies that of the U.S. Treasury, and called for a halt to the flow of resources from Latin America to the industrialised countries, presently standing at $32 billion per year. Their main demands were:

1. For a 3% drop in interest rates within a year (though recognising that a welcome 3% drop had already happened in the previous 15 months).

2. For roughly half as much again new commercial bank lending as was called for by Baker.

3. For banks to cease their practice of charging more indebted countries higher interest rates.
4. For a 15–20% increase in lending from the multilateral agencies such as the World Bank.
5. For some interest charges to be added to the loans, rather than paid in cash.
6. For a special issue of IMF loans (Special Drawing Rights) for debtor countries.
7. For greater compensation, through the IMF, for lost earnings when commodity prices fall.

In addition to this consensus approach, certain Latin American governments have taken unilateral action in response to their individual difficulties. Bolivia effectively defaulted on its debts in 1984. Next Peru, facing an impossible balance of payments problem, announced that it would refuse to pay more than 10% of its export earnings to pay its debt bill. Then Brazil flew in the face of IMF anger by breaking off negotiations with the Fund and launching a $2.5 billion anti-poverty drive. And then Mexico, hit by the falling price of oil — its chief export — announced that it would only recognise an interest rate of 6%.

9. The African Governments

The African approach to date has been more to cry from the heart than to negotiate a new deal for debt. They have recognised their own very weak bargaining power, have admitted their faults and have undertaken to 'put their own own houses in order' (along IMF lines), if only the West would give them a leg-up out of the debt crisis.

For most African governments a threat of default would not generate too much fear amongst the banking community. In effect Sudan and some other countries have defaulted for years, but these actions won't precipitate a new economic approach. Some governments (notably Tanzania) argue more strongly for international reforms, and Nigeria (sub-Saharan Africa's largest debtor, and an oil exporter) has followed Mexico and Peru's lead by unilaterally reducing its debt repayments, setting a debt payment ceiling of 30% of its export earnings.[12] But most of the 50 countries of Africa have agreed to take the IMF medicine. Twenty-eight countries had introduced programmes of economic reform.[13] The combined debt of the continent has risen to $158 billion (1985 World Bank estimates) with debt service charges (interest plus repayments) of $20 billion a year, or a quarter of all export earnings.

At the UN Special Session on Africa in May 1986, the African governments owned up to their share of the blame for the crisis and spelt out a detailed reform programme.[14] Western leaders have welcomed this as a 'new spirit of realism' on the part of the African leaders, but as yet little new practical support has been offered.

10. Lever and Huhne: *Debt and Danger*

An imaginative and plausible reform programme for the international economic system is constructed by two British economists (Lord Lever and Christopher Huhne) in their 1985 report *Debt and Danger*.[15] Their starting point is that the present flow of finance from developing to Western countries, caused by high interest rates, should be stemmed. This demands some $20–30 billion per year of new resources. The significance of the report is in describing how these resources — tiny in comparison to the Marshall Plan that rescued post-war Europe — could be mustered. They counter the claim that any new 'Marshall Plan' would rekindle world inflation by pointing out that as long as the new funds went into *productive* investment, they would rekindle world growth without triggering inflation. Two of the proposals they outline are:

a) For Northern governments to guarantee new commercial bank loans to developing countries. In exchange the banks would have to agree to write off a portion of their doubtful debts each year over a long period. This would also give debtor countries a good reason not to default and consequently would give the banks time to work off their bad loans.

b) An increase in funds committed via the World Bank and IMF with a concentration of those funds on productive investment and improvement in living standards of the poor — so IMF conditionality would shift from austerity to productivity.

Notes and references

Setting the Scene

1 Richard Jolly, Deputy Director, Unicef, speaking at the Society for International Development, Rome, July 1985.
2 Unicef, *Survey of the Impact of Recession on Children*, 1983.
3 Unicef, op. cit.
4 Oxfam, *An Unnatural Disaster: Drought in N. East Brazil*, 1984.
5 Belinda Coote, *Debt and Poverty: A Case Study of Jamaica*, Oxfam 1985.
6 Nick Cater, *Sudan: the Roots of Famine*, Oxfam, 1986.
7 Unicef, *Within Human Reach*, 1985.
8 Oxfam, West Africa Field Office Annual Report 1985/86.
9 World Bank, *Poverty and Hunger: Issues and Options for Food Security in Developing Countries*, March 1986.
10 FAO estimates

Aid

1 ODA, *British Overseas Aid In 1985*.
2 Nick Cater, *Sudan: the Roots of Famine*, Oxfam 1986.
3 Personal communication with author, May 1986.
4 ODA, *British Aid Statistics*, 1985.
5 Michael Lipton, Institute of Development Studies, University of Sussex, in correspondence with author, July 1986.
6 Foreign Affairs Committee, *Famine in Africa*, 1985.
7 ODA, *British Overseas Aid in 1985*, op cit.
8 Ibid — author's calculation based on ODA figures.
9 ODA, *British Aid Statistics 1979–83*.
10 ODA memorandum to the OECD, 1984.
11 Baroness Young, FCO Minister, to Director of Oxfam, 27.12.84.
12 Oxfam memorandum to the British Government on the need for development aid to Ethiopia, April 1985.
13 ODA, *British Aid Statistics*, 1985.
14 World Bank, *Towards Sustained Development in Sub-Saharan Africa*, 1984.
15 UNCTAD report, May 1985.
16 Sir William Ryrie, "Managing an Aid Programme", IDS Bulletin, April 1986.
17 Ibid.
18 Oxfam, West Africa Field Office Annual Report 1985/86.
19 Henrietta Search, *EEC Emergency Food Aid Measures*, Oxfam, 1986.
20 Timothy Raison, speech in Dyfed 20.6.86.
21 ODA, *British Overseas Aid 1985*.
22 Suzanne Williams, *"Women in Development"* paper, Oxfam 1983.
23 Oxfam, Zambia Field Office Annual Report 1985/86.
24 Unicef, *Within Human Reach*, 1985.
25 Foreign Affairs Committee, 1985, op. cit.
26 Timothy Raison, *Hansard*, 11.5.1986.

27 *UK Aid for African Agriculture*, report of the working party established by the All Party Parliamentary Group on Overseas Development, ODI, October 1985.
28 Unicef, *Within Human Reach*, 1985.
29 ODA, *British Aid Statistics*, 1985.
30 *New Scientist*, 4.4.1985.
31 *The Times*, 25.3.1985.
32 World Bank, *Poverty and Hunger: Issues and Options for Food Security in Developing Countries*, March 1986.
33 Oxfam, Brazil Field Office Annual Report 1985.

Trade

1 Brian Hartley, internal Oxfam report, June 1984.
2 World Bank tables. World Development Report, 1985.
3 World Bank index of non-oil commodities:
coffee, cocoa, tea, maize, rice, wheat, sorghum, soya beans, groundnuts, palm oil, coconut oil, copra, groundnut oil, soya bean meal, sugar, beef, bananas, oranges, cotton, jute, rubber, tobacco, logs, copper, tin, nickel, bauxite, aluminium, iron ore, manganese ore, lead, zinc and phosphate.
4 *Zambia*: Digest of Statistics; *Sudan:* Bank of Sudan Economic and Financial Statistics; *Malawi*: Economic reports; *Bangladesh:* Monthly Statistics Bulletin of Bangladesh.
5 *World Bank News,* January 1986. Index prices of 33 non-oil commodities fell 18% from the period 1979/81 to the close of 1984.
6 Estimated from World Bank tables, World Development Report, 1985. Export earnings of countries whose GNP per capita was lesss than $2000 in 1983. Over half this was primary commodities, so an 18% fall in the price index represents a loss of approximately $40 billion per year.
7 Unicef, *Within Human Reach*, 1985.
8 *International Herald Tribune*, 21.3.1986.
9 FAO Production and Trade Year books and Commodity Reviews.
10 Ibid.
11 Edouard Saouma, Director General, FAO, *International Herald Tribune*, 29 April 1985.
12 FAO Production and Trade Yearbooks.
13 Frances Stewart, paper to the Other Economic Summit, 1985.
14 Campaign Co-operative, *World in Your Coffee Cup*, 1980.
15 Nigel Twose, ex Oxfam Field Director, *Earthscan*, February, 1985.
16 FAO Production and Trade Year books.
17 Oxfam, West Africa Field Office Annual Report, 1985/86.
18 World Bank, *Poverty and Hunger: Issues and options for Food Security in Developing Countries*, March 1986.
19 Oxfam, op. cit.
20 Economist Intelligence Unit, Quarterly Report No 4, 1985.
21 Ibid.
22 *The Economist*, 15.6.1986.
23 *Financial Times*, 15.4.1985.
24 Oxfam, Caribbean Field Office Annual Report, 1985/86.
25 Nick Cater, *Sudan: the Roots of Famine*, Oxfam 1986.
26 World Development Movement, *New Deal for the Poorest*, 1986.
27 World Bank Annual Report, 1985.
28 Leelananda de Silva, *Weighted Scales*, NGLS, 1986.
29 *Financial Times*, 29.10.84.
30 World Development Movement, op. cit.
31 Letter from Mrs. Thatcher to Judith Stinton, 18.4.1986.
32 Leelananda de Silva, op. cit.
33 *Economic and Political Weekly*, Bombay, xiii no. 37, 16.9.1978.
34 Leelananda de Silva, op. cit.

35 World Development Movement, op. cit.
36 1981 figures based on comparison between figures in *New Deal for the Poorest* (see note 35) and World Bank tables. (see note 6).
37 *The Guardian*, 6.12.1985.
38 *Financial Times*, 22.10.1985.
39 Leelananda de Silva, op. cit.
40 *The Guardian*, 27.3.1986.
41 World Development Movement, op. cit.

Agriculture

1 *Daily Telegraph*, 10.4.1986.
2 World Bank, *World Development Report, 1986*.
3 *Daily Telegraph*, 4.7.1986.
4 *Hansard*, 6.2.1986.
5 Adrian Moyes, *How Farming in Europe Affects the Third World Poor*, Oxfam, 1986.
6 Ibid.
7 Ibid.
8 Keith Schreider, *International Herald Tribune*, 6.8.1986.
9 Adrian Moyes, op. cit.
10 Belinda Coote, *Debt and Poverty: a case study of Jamaica*, Oxfam 1985.
11 Ibid.
12 "CAP and its impact on the Third World", ODI Briefing Paper, June 1986.
13 *The Times*, 28.3.86.

Debt

1 *The Guardian*, 21.3.1985.
2 Institute for International Economics, *African Debt and Financing*, p. 202. 1986.
3 S. Griffiths-Jones and L. Nichols, *"New Directions in debt Crisis Management"*, Paper 1986.
4 Unpublished OECD figures.
5 Anthony Sampson, *The Money Lenders*, 1986.
6 Harold Lever and Christopher Huhne, *Debt and Danger*, Penguin special, 1985.
7 *Financial Times*, 3.10.1985.
8 World Bank, *Towards Sustained Development in sub-Saharan Africa*, 1984.
9 S. Griffiths-Jones and L. Nichols, op. cit.
10 Leelananda de Silva, *Weighted Scales*, NGLS, 1980.
11 Keith Griffin, *The Debt Crisis and the Poor*.
12 *The Guardian*, 10.3.86.
13 Harold Lever and Christopher Huhne, op. cit.
14 Oxfam, "The Debt Crisis, Oxfam's concern for the poor", a Hungry for Change Brief, 1985.
15 Oxfam, Zambia Field Office Annual Report, 1985/86.
16 Ibid.
17 Ibid.
18 Ibid.
19 S. Griffiths-Jones and L. Nichols, op. cit.
20 Harold Lever and Christopher Huhne, op. cit.
21 Institute for International Economics, op. cit.
22 Ibid.
23 World Bank figures.
24 World Bank, *Towards Sustained Development in sub-Saharan Africa*, 1986 and *Financing Adjustment with Growth in sub-Saharan Africa*, 1986.
25 Institute for International Economics, op. cit.
26 World Bank, op. cit.
27 *The Guardian*, 21.3.1985.
28 Citicorp advertisement reproduced in "The Debt Crisis: Oxfam's concerns for the poor", Oxfam 1985.

29 Harold Lever and Christopher Huhne, op. cit.
30 *The Debt Crisis and the World Economy*, report by a Commonwealth Group of Experts, July 1984.
31 *The Guardian*, 2.8.1985.
32 Based on, Belinda Coote, *Debt and Poverty: a case study of Jamaica*, Oxfam, 1985.
33 Oxfam project application JMA PP 14/85/86.
34 Based on author's interview with Audrey Bronstein, Oxfam's Country Representative in Lima, July 1986.
35 World Bank, *Financing Adjustment with Growth in sub-Saharan Africa*, 1986.
36 Paula Park and Tony Jackson, *Lands of Plenty, Lands of Scarcity*, Oxfam, 1985.
37 *The Guardian*, 19.8.1985.
38 *The Guardian*, 24.4.1985.
39 *The Guardian*, 13.8.1985.
40 *New Statesman*, 17.1.1986.
41 *Financial Times*, 7.1.1986.
42 *The Times*, 6.1.1986.
43 *International Herald Tribune*, 29.12.1985.
44 *The Guardian*, 2.4.1985.
45 UNCTAD Report, Summer 1985.
46 Harold Lever and Christopher Huhne, op. cit.

Arms

1 Willy Brandt, *World Armament and World Hunger*, Gollancz, 1986.
2 *The Lancet*, 7.12.1985, pp. 1287–9.
3 Inga Thorssen, IDS Bulletin, October 1985.
4 *World Military and Social Expenditure, 1985*.
5 Unicef, *Within Human Reach*, 1985.
6 Based on, Dianna Melrose, *Nicaragua: the Threat of a Good Example?*, Oxfam, 1985.
7 Deger and Smith, IDS Bulletin, October 1985.
8 Calculated from figures in World Bank, *World Development Report 1986.*
9 World Bank, *World Development Report 1985.*
10 Chris Smith, *IDS Bulletin,* October 1985.
11 Harold Lever and Christopher Huhne, *Debt and Danger*, Penguin Special, 1985.
12 Inga Thorssen, op. cit.
13 SIPRI, *World Armament and Disarmament 1985.*
14 Ibid.
15 Campaign Against the Arms Trade, Newsletter, 13.12.1985.
16 *Hansard*, written answer by the Minister of State for Defence Procurement, 16.12.1985.
17 Harold Lever and Christopher Huhne, op. cit.
18 SIPRI, op. cit. and Chris Smith, op. cit.
19 Ibid, SIPRI.
20 Ibid.
21 Deger and Smith, op. cit.
22 *South*, November 1985.
23 David Bull, *The Poverty of Diplomacy*, Oxfam 1983.
24 *World Military and Social Expenditure 1985*.

Appendix II

1 *Financial Times*, 24.5.1985.
2 Letter from Derek Glecton to Oxfam.
3 *Financial Times*, 24.5.1985.
4 Foreign Affairs Committee Supply Estimates 1982–83.
5 HMG White Paper on public expenditure, January 1986.

Appendix III

1 *North–South; A Programme for Survival* & *Common Crisis; Cooperation for World Recovery*, Reports of the Independent Commission on International Development Issues under the Chairmanship of Willy Brandt, Pan Books, World Affairs Series, 1980 and 1983.
2 Celso Furtado, *No to Recession and Unemployment*, Third World Foundation for Social and Economic Studies, London, 1984.
3 UNCTAD, *The Least Developed Countries*, 1984.
4 *Translating Recovery into Growth: an UNCTAD View*, report to the World Bank and IMF meetings, April, 1985.
5 World Bank, *World Development Report 1985*, July 1985.
6 World Bank, *Towards Sustained Development in Sub-Saharan Africa*, September, 1984.
7 World Bank, *Poverty and Hunger.*
8 *The Debt Crisis and the World Economy*, report by a Commonwealth Group of Experts chaired by Lord Lever.
9 Unicef, *Within Human Reach*, December, 1985.
10 *The Times*, 30.9.1985, *The Observer*, 6.10.1985, *The Guardian*, 7.10.1985, *International Herald Tribune*, 6.11.1985.
11 *The Guardian*, 13.12.1985.
12 Financial Times, 13 & 18.12.1985.
13 Harold Lever & Christopher Huhne, *Debt and Danger*, Penguin Special, 1985.

Further reading

Aid

British Overseas Aid, (Annual Reports), Overseas Development Administration.
UK Aid for African Agriculture, All Party Parliamentary Group on Overseas Development, Overseas Development Institute, 1985.
Real Aid, A Strategy for Britain, Independent Group on British Aid, 1982.
Sudan, The Roots of Famine, Nick Cater, Oxfam, 1986.

Trade

New Deal for the Poorest, World Development Movement, 1986.
Feeding the Few, Susan George, IPS, 1979.
Food First, Frances Moore Lappe & Joe Collins, Souvenir Press.

Agriculture

How Farming in Europe Affects the Third World Poor, Adrian Moyes, Oxfam, 1986.
World Development Report 1986, World Bank.
Against the Grain, T. Jackson & D. Eade, Oxfam, 1982.

Debt

Debt and Danger, Harold Lever and Christopher Huhne, Penguin Special, 1985.
Within Human Reach, Unicef 1985.
Debt & Poverty: a Case Study of Jamaica, Belinda Coote, Oxfam, 1985.

Arms

World Armament and World Hunger: a Call to Action, Willy Brandt, Gollancz, 1986.
World Armament and Disarmament, SIPRI, 1985.
Nicaragua: the Threat of a Good Example?, Dianna Melrose, Oxfam, 1985.

General

North South: a Programme for Survival, Report of the Brandt Commission, Pan, 1980.
Common Crisis: Cooperation for World Recovery, Report of the Brandt Commission, Pan, 1983.
Aid is not Enough, Independent Group on British Aid, 1984.
Missed Opportunities, Independent Group on British Aid, 1986.